THE MENTAL GAME

The Inner Game of Bowling

By George Allen

Illustrated by Joanne Allen

TECH-ED PUBLISHING CO.
P. O. BOX 4
DEERFIELD, IL 60015

ACKNOWLEDGEMENTS: A special thanks to:

my wife Joanne, for Editorial Assistance, and for illustrating the book.

the AMF and Brunswick Corporations, for their support of our books.

Chuck Pezzano, for the many rewarding conversations we have had.

the publishers of BOWLING, THE WOMAN BOWLER, and the BOWLERS JOURNAL, for the numerous articles which have helped me.

Dick Ritger, who has one of the best mental games of anyone who has ever bowled.

many professional bowlers who have shared their ideas with me.

the people who have purchased THE ENCYCLOPEDIA OF BOWLING INSTRUCTION.

members of the FAIR LANES Corporation, especially Wally Hall, Bob Haux, and Pete Santora.

Richard, Karen, and Barbara

Helen and Howell Babbitt

Third Printing, 1991

Published in the United States of America

Library of Congress Number: 83-050980

ISBN: 0-933554-18-4

TABLE OF CONTENTS

PURPOSE AND OVERVIEW OF THE BOOK

The purpose of this book is to explore the mental aspect of bowling. Although bowling is widely conceived to be purely a physical game of rolling the ball down the lane, it should be obvious that such is not the case. Bowlers who achieve and maintain high averages have developed both a solid mental and physical game.

The serious or competitive bowler is the primary focus of this book. Although the mental game is important at all average levels, it becomes increasingly important at higher average levels, or in competitive situations.

Bowling suffers from the image that no physical or mental skills are required to bowl well. Do not be fooled by the ease with which top bowlers perform. All professional athletes make their activity seem effortless. Their skills are hidden behind what look like routine movements and actions. Yet an expert can easily detect the requirements for top level performance, in bowling and in any other sport. Definite mental and physical skills are required to achieve a high average and bowl well on a consistent basis.

I assume that you have a good physical game, you have the ability to deliver the ball in well-timed, consistent, and natural manner. If that's not true, you may wish to develop your physical game by reading and using three other books I wrote, called THE ENCYCLOPEDIA OF BOWLING INSTRUCTION.

Physical skills are usually the only ones taught. Mental skills are much less tangible, and cannot be as readily seen or assessed as physical skills. Yet, mental skills are far more important than physical skills for top level performance.

The mental game is a skill that can be identified and developed. It is independent from but related to the ability to roll the ball well. The mental game can be learned; it can be taught, which is the purpose of this book. Devoting your attentions only to the physical game places a ceiling on your performance that is far below what can be achieved with a good mental game and a good physical game.

THE MENTAL GAME is designed to be used as a reference book. You need not read the book in the order that the material is presented. Therefore, each page contains the full title of the topic, allowing you to find any material by fanning the pages.

I recommend, however, that you read sections 1, 2, and 3 first. They establish the foundation for understanding the other sections. These first three topics are: The Mental Game; Conscious & Subconscious Minds; and Developing Subconscious Competence. After you have a clear understanding of these topics, the remaining areas can be read in the order they appeal to you.

The mental side of bowling draws heavily from many specialized areas of study, including: psychology, anatomy, psychiatry, physics, biology, and even the computer sciences.

THE MENTAL GAME deals with such specific subjects as self-hypnosis, hypnosis, psycho-cybernetics, cybernetics, and the mechanics and operation of the mind. These areas are very broad, but the presentation is restricted to aspects of these fields directly related to the mental game of bowling.

It is not possible to treat all these subjects fully in THE MENTAL GAME. It is also necessary to avoid technical terms where possible, and to restate the material in easy-to-read language. I have tried to do this. For you who wish to go into greater depth, the Bibliography contains references to books which provide more detailed and technical background.

The sections are presented as discrete parts, but overlap exists. There is some intentional duplication between sections, when material or concepts are appropriate for more than one section.

The words YOU and SELF are very important to the development of a sound mental game. YOU must take total control (SELF-control) of the process which develops your mental game; YOU are responsible to initiate (SELF-start) the process which establishes your frame of mind for entering competition; and YOU must learn the ways to regulate (SELF-regulate) your mental and physical games for top performance. YOU are the most important person in determining how well you develop and maintain your mental skills.

The mental aspect of sports performances has been called "the inner game". Timothy Gallwey is credited with developing this phrase, as a result of his two books: THE INNER GAME OF TENNIS and THE INNER GAME OF GOLF. Both books are in the Bibliography and highly recommended.

The inner game concept refers to the subconscious mind. To illustrate the concept of the conscious and subconscious minds, two characters have been created: MYCON (for MY CONscious mind), and MYSUB (for MY SUBconscious) mind. There are over 25 illustrations in THE MENTAL GAME, to highlight points of discussion.

Development of the mental game is a never-ending process. You cannot hope to forever eliminate the mental game as an aspect of competition. Pressure situations will always arise and you must be able to mentally respond to such situations. An attack of nerves or anxiety is always a real possibility, unless you are in control of your mental game, one of the objectives of THE MENTAL GAME.

Confidence in your mental game is an elusive quality; here one game and gone the next. You must stay on top of your mental game, viewing it as something worthy of your highest level of attention. You can develop a mental game that is your biggest source of strength in the many critical situations which separate the good from the great in any sport.

MENTAL GROWTH HAS NO BOUNDS. As you age, your physical game may stop improving or may even decline. Your strength may leave you. You may develop any number of physical ailments that would reduce your physical fitness. BUT, YOUR MENTAL GAME NEED NEVER DECLINE. IT SHOULD GROW WITH AGE. I hope this book will help you in your quest for a winning mental game.

DR. GEORGE R. ALLEN,
Tempe, Arizona

AUTHOR'S NOTE: This book has been produced completely by computer. This allowed me to use larger type, spread the words out, and avoid any hyphenation at the end of a line. The result should be a book that is very easy to read.

COMING ATTRACTION
MYCON VERSUS MYSUB

Tonight and every night
At your local bowling center

The mental game is a struggle between the conscious and subconscious minds.

--- PHYSICAL ABILITY PLUS MENTAL ABILITY EQUALS WINNING ABILITY. ---

When you are physically able to deliver the ball in a natural, consistent, and well-timed manner, you have the foundation upon which you can build your average to your maximum potential. At that point the mental game comes into play as the single factor which will either allow you to take your average to a higher level or keep it below your full potential. Physical ability plus mental ability leads to high-average bowling. Both are necessary.

The mental game has been called "the inner game" by Timothy Gallwey, author of THE INNER GAME OF TENNIS. He states: "The inner game takes place in the mind of the player. It is played against such obstacles as lapses in concentration, nervousness, self-doubt, and self-condemnation....It is played to overcome all habits of mind which inhibit excellence in performance."

The mental game is one that is played against yourself. YOU ARE YOUR OWN OPPONENT IN THE MENTAL GAME; YOU ARE COMPETING WITH YOURSELF. The physical game, on the other hand is played against your opponent. Thus, you really might have two competitors each time you bowl, yourself and your opponent. The solution is to get your mental game working for and not against you.

The physical game is far more stable than the mental game. The mental game can have wide fluctuations. Pressure situations can get you nervous and tense; you can become anxious and doubt your ability to perform under pressure; you can think too much of failing or winning, and not enough about proper execution, etc. Your mental state could vary greatly from day to day, or from hour to hour, with particularly high or low mental swings in competition.

Therefore, you have to pay close attention to your mental game at all times if you want to achieve your maximum potential on the lanes. Since the mental game is so volatile, your goal is to stabilize it so that there are no wide fluctuations. The ultimate goal is both a stable physical game and a stable mental game, both under your control at all times.

You can become the master of your mind, body, and emotions. To do so is to develop the mental game to the level that your body and mind are working for you in all competitive situations.

The illustration on the outside back cover provides a general picture of the relationship between the mental and physical games, relating each one to Low Average, Average, and High Average performance levels.

A common misconception held by many bowlers is the mistaken assumption that bowling is largely a physical game at all average levels. A related assumption is that all one has to do to achieve a higher average is to bowl more games, to practice. This is not true.

The importance of the mental side of your game increases as your skill level increases. More accurately, to increase your average it is necessary to know much more about bowling (equipment selection, angle and delivery adjustments, mathematically based spare and strike adjustment systems, etc.). High-average bowling is definitely a thinking game, far more than it is a physical game of simply rolling the ball down the lane.

Good bowling has always been more of a mental than a physical game. Yet the game has been perceived as having very little mental or intellectual content. Perhaps this image of the game has been created by those who promote bowling as an easy game that anyone can do. While anyone can roll a ball down a lane, and anyone could bowl a high game or series on occasion (more by luck than by skill), not anyone can bowl well on a consistent basis unless he or she has a good mental and physical game.

The distinction needs to be made between rolling a ball down a lane and good bowling. There is a difference. Although both are in the strict sense of the word bowling, the high average bowler is bowling well, while the other person is simply rolling a ball. Consistently good bowlers have a well-developed mental game.

Actually, there are two distinct parts of the mental game. One relates to the conscious decisions you have to make each time you bowl. The other relates to your emotional state of mind .

Some of the conscious decisions which form one side of the mental game include: What equipment should you use, in terms of ball surface, balance, and ball fit? What strike line or angle will work best on the lanes at this point in time? How are the ball and lane interacting? What angle, equipment or delivery adjustments will have to be made to score well? Are there any unusual lane conditions that have to be taken into account? What approach position and target on the lanes will you use for every spare you have to convert? These are only a few of the conscious decisions you have to make, and make them correctly, if you are to achieve a high average.

On the emotional side of the mental game are such factors as ability to control your temper, handle pressure and tension situations, relax, concentrate, accept wins and losses, maintain a positive attitude, etc. These emotional factors may all come into play while you are bowling, and all will affect your success on the lanes.

There is a "physical balance" requirement as you deliver the ball. There is also a "mental balance" which is necessary during your delivery. If your body is in perfect balance and your mind is also in balance, your game is as ideal as it can be.

It is the purpose of this book to discuss these emotional factors which influence your mental game, both at the conscious and subconscious levels. The objective is the development of a winning mental game. All sections have as their purpose some improvement in your mental outlook, your mental state during competition, your attitudes and emotions; in short, the development of mental competence.

A good mental approach to both winning and losing is essential to the long-run development of a sound mental game. If you have physical ailments, obviously you would administer to those needs; you would use "physical first aid" techniques. But what about times when you have mental ailments, following either a loss or poor performance? Would you consider the use of "mental first aid" on those mental problems? You should. The development of mental ailments is just as likely (if not more likely) than the development of physical ailments.

The possibility of developing mental ailments following either a win or a loss is very real. Therefore, the concept of mental first aid should be explored and understood if you wish to develop a healthy mental game.

A person who LOSES may develop an incorrect mental attitude or frame of mind that could later make it very difficult for him or her to win. On the other hand, he or she could WIN and still develop a mental attitude that makes it difficult for a later win. Thus, attitudes after each competitive situation must be "tended to" to insure that the result is growth in good mental health.

A win can lead one to believe that winning is too easy, particularly if it comes early in that persons competitive career. A quick win could lead to an inflated opinion of one's talents. It could lead to placement of personal pressure on oneself, trying too hard the next time you compete to prove something to yourself or to others. An inflated ego can alienate the winner from other competitors, leading to a poor mental attitude.

The proper mental attitude after a win is just as important as your attitude after a loss. Letting yourself down gradually after a win, learning to accept it gracefully, putting the win in proper perspective, are all parts of developing a winning mental game.

A loss can have the same detrimental effects if you are not careful, if you do not apply mental first aid techniques. Realistically, you will lose many more competitive situations than you will win, if you evaluate your performance only on whether you win the tournament or not. Expecting to win each time is asking too much of yourself. Trying to win each time is, of course, your goal in each competitive situation. However, learning how to accept your losses can go a long way toward developing the kind of mental game that will lead to increasingly better performances.

One way to "win" each competitive situation you enter is to change the way you judge your performance. Judge your performance on how well you tried, how well you executed your shots, your mental attitude during competition. Then, if you try as hard as you can, and maintain the proper perspective during competition, you will never "fail".

Learn how to let yourself down gracefully after a loss; but a better mental approach is to judge your performance based upon how well you tried. If you have executed your shots as well as you can, then there is no reason to judge your performance as a failure simply because you did not win. Thinking in terms of being a failure is not only an attitude detrimental to your mental game, but is not correct. Many times you will execute well and still not finish in first place. At other times you will not execute well and yet you will win. Learn how to accept both situations and each will lead to improvement in your mental game. Eventually, this improved mental game will lead to continuously good performances each time you compete. Consistent performances will lead to good finishes and your share of wins. Let the wins happen when they will.

There is a direct relationship between the condition of the body and the condition of the mind. Good physical conditioning leads to good mental conditioning. Improving your cardiovascular system (your heart and related organs) can lead to very dramatic improvements in mental powers.

This relationship between physical and mental conditioning is obvious to anyone who is informed about athletic conditioning programs. Many bowlers, aware of this connection, like to jog to keep in good physical and mental shape. The act of jogging is good for the mind as well as the body. Several factors account for this mental benefit from a physical activity.

Jogging (and other physical exercise) causes an increased flow of oxygen to all parts of the body, including the mind. The mind uses from 20% to 30% of the oxygen in the body. Therefore, mental stimulation is a direct result of physical stimulation, or increased flow of oxygen to the body.

Jogging also teaches you patience. If you are out for a 3 to 10 mile run, you have to learn how to pace yourself. You cannot force the body to exceed its natural limits (although you can learn to expand these limits). This patience comes in handy during long tournament formats, where you must also pace yourself both mentally and physically. You must keep making good shots, keep making your spares, until the strikes come. You need to avoid mental impatience or stagnation. If you are not performing very well, you have to learn to "wait it out", to ride out the bad streak until the good shots come. If you become impatient you are likely to get down on yourself, causing you to perform at a lower level than you are capable of achieving. Patience is an asset to any athlete, especially to a bowler who is in a slump.

The physical act of jogging teaches you mind control. It also stimulates fresh thinking and creates new ideas, preventing your mind from becoming stale. I find that the ideas flow so freely when I am jogging that I sometimes take a tape recorder along to capture the ideas before they are lost. This mental stimulation is a direct result of the increased oxygen flow to the brain.

The physiological changes in the body brought about by increased oxygen flow are well documented. Such findings suggest that any serious bowler who wants to achieve his or her full potential should use physical activity to stimulate mental activity. Get more oxygen flowing through your body and you are developing mental alertness, mental skill.

Of course, other types of physical activity can have the same beneficial effects as jogging. As long as you are improving the flow of oxygen, you are assisting mental activities. Select the form of physical activity that appeals to you and engage in it on a regular basis. The training effect only occurs when the physical activity is performed regularly.

Physical activity also leads to decreased stress. The body benefits from reduced stress in many ways, particularly while you are bowling. Bowling is a game of relaxed muscles, not tensed muscles. Anything you can do to reduce tension and stress will pave the way for improved performance. Physical activity will relax the muscles. (The subjects of stress, pressure, tension and anxiety will be addressed in later sections.)

Perhaps one of the biggest problems facing bowlers is their apparent lack of concern for their physical health, which as we have just seen has a direct bearing on their mental health. Too many of them drink and smoke to excess, and do not have a planned program for maintaining physical fitness. Many do not get the proper amount of sleep; they do not get the right amount or type of food; they do not take care of themselves. If they do not take care of themselves physically, then they are not taking care of themselves mentally. And, as previously stated, the mental game is far more important at high-average competitive levels of play.

Many bowlers DO take care of themselves. They show concern for physical fitness. Many know the positive benefits of good physical health, and they develop good exercise and diet habits. These winners are rewarded for their concern for their bodies.

There are, of course, many more facets to the mental game. These will be discussed in other sections. If bowling is ever going to achieve the status of other professional sports, the existence of the mental and intellectual sides of the game must be both understood and accepted. To remove the mental part of the game, to ignore its existence, to consider bowling as only a physical activity, is demeaning to the sport and will continue to prevent bowling from ever achieving recognition as a professional sporting activity as well as a recreational activity. To imply that anyone can bowl (well), and that all one has to do to improve is to bowl more games, is to treat bowling as a game that requires no mental or physical skills to master.

With a good physical game (the ability to deliver the ball in a natural, consistent and well-timed manner) you have the potential to achieve a high average. With a good mental game you may be able to score well even when your physical game is lacking. You may not be able to reach your full potential until your physical game improves, but you could score well. With both a good physical game and a good mental game, there is no practical limit to what average level you could reach. With that in mind, we can now continue the study of the requirements for a good mental game.

	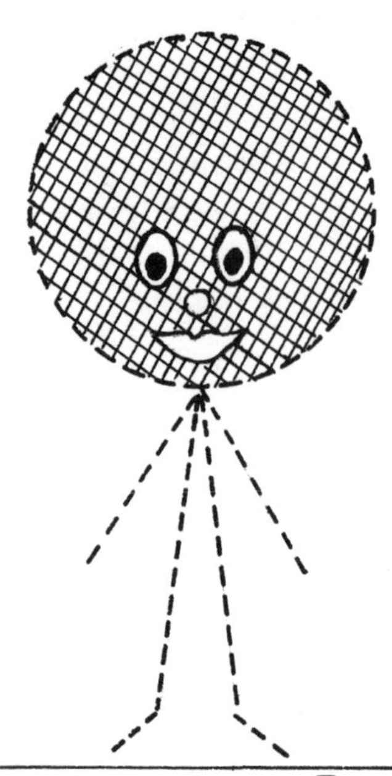
MYCON	**MYSUB**
IS JUDGMENTAL	IS NON-JUDGMENTAL
CAN EVALUATE	CANNOT EVALUATE
CAN REASON	CANNOT REASON
IS THE TEACHER	IS THE STUDENT
IS THE THINKER	IS THE DOER
GIVES COMMANDS	FOLLOWS COMMANDS
LEARNS THINGS	STORES LEARNING
CAN CHOOSE	CANNOT CHOOSE
TEACHES MUSCLES	DIRECTS MUSCLES

--- EVERY HUMAN SKILL IS FIRST LEARNED UNDER THE CRITICAL GUIDANCE AND SUPERVISION OF THE CONSCIOUS MIND. ---

The existence of both a conscious and subconscious mind has been known for some time. Therefore, this section will be brief, only touching on both aspects of the mind long enough to set the foundation for later sections. Another purpose for this section is to introduce two characters who "star" in the illustrations in this book.

Man is blessed with a conscious mind, capable of reasoning. It is this aspect of the mind, and the extent to which man can reason that separates him from all other animals. The power of reasoning is one of the most important differences between the conscious and subconscious minds. The subconscious mind cannot reason on its own.

Jack Heise, in HOW YOU CAN BOWL BETTER USING SELF-HYPNOSIS, considers the power of reasoning as the basis for both hypnosis and self-hypnosis. He states, "The basic theory of hypnosis is the fact that the conscious mind has the exclusive power to reason and the subconscious has no power to reason and accepts everything it receives as truth.

The power of reasoning means the ability to make choices. The conscious mind is capable of choosing from any number of alternatives, and is capable of creating the alternatives. The subconscious mind does not make choices, it only follows the instructions which it has been given by the conscious mind. The subconscious mind responds in an automatic manner, similar to a conditioned response. No choices can be made by the subconscious.

The conscious mind can direct the destiny of the body in which it is found. It has the power to make a wide range of decisions, any one of which could greatly change the destiny of the person, the body and mind. The subconscious mind does not direct, it follows; It acts upon command from the conscious mind; It issues no commands.

The conscious mind has the power to evaluate. It can compare and rate any number of variables. Evaluation requires judgment. The conscious mind can execute judgment, whereas, the subconscious mind can make no judgments on its own. It questions nothing. It reacts, similar to the way a computer does, doing exactly what it is programmed to do and nothing more or less.

Maxwell Maltz, in PSYCHO-CYBERNETICS, suggests that the science of Cybernetics has provided proof that the subconscious mind is no mind at all, "but a mechanism--a goal-striving, servo-mechanism consisting of the brain and nervous system, which is used by and directed by the mind". He continues that man does not have two minds, only one. The subconscious is, in his opinion, simply an automatic, goal-striving machine.

Psycho-cybernetic concepts relate the brain and the nervous system of the body to the functions of a computer, another type of servo-mechanism. Psycho-cybernetics also explains the behavior of humans as though each person has a machine-like mechanism which is goal-seeking. That mechanism is the human brain, more specifically, the subconscious part of the brain.

His assessment of the existence of only one mind, plus a machine-like mechanism, is consistent with the concept of two minds (a conscious and subconscious), except that he downgrades the classification of the subconscious from a "mind" to a machine. Since the subconscious acts so much like a computer, I cannot find fault with his analogy. In fact, it is helpful to think of the subconscious mind as a robot-like mechanism ready to serve the conscious mind.

Lager and Kraft, authors of MENTAL JUDO, think that there are two conscious minds, one talking to you in a confused, shakey voice, and the other in a consistent and confident voice. The problem, as seen by these authors, is learning how to cope with both of these conscious minds.

Lager and Kraft have termed one of the conscious minds the Analytic Mind, and the other the Emotional Mind. The objective, according to these two researchers, is to get the Analytic Mind and the Emotional Mind together. This concept also has validity and is similar to the concept of the Inner Game as originally described by Timothy Gallwey. (Gallwey's concept is discussed in Section 1, THE MENTAL GAME.)

The conscious mind can call upon the muscles at any time, commanding them to do its bidding. My conscious mind is telling my fingers to type this sentence. My subconscious mind is actually doing the typing, since it is not possible to type with any degree of speed if you have to consciously look at the keys. You can type consciously, which is called the "hunt and pick system". But touch typing is a subconscious skill, taught by the conscious mind, but executed by the subconscious.

Every human skill is first learned under the critical guidance and supervision of the conscious mind. However, once the skill is learned by the subconscious mind, all the conscious mind has to do is issue the command and the activity will take place. For example, once you learn how to walk, all the conscious mind has to do is tell the subconscious to walk, and you walk. The conscious mind is free to do anything it wants while you walk. The subconscious directs the walking, following the patterns of muscle movement taught to it by the conscious mind.

The subconscious mind can repeat muscle movements it has been taught, over and over again. It cannot change the instructions or directions given by the conscious mind; it obediently follows the command without question.

The subconscious mind is a storehouse of information. Some people believe that everything the conscious mind senses or sees is somehow stored in the subconscious mind. The only problem is to be able to retrieve the information when it is needed.

The subconscious mind can be taught a wide variety of things, involving the most intricate and detailed muscle movement. Walking, talking, singing, dancing, typing, playing a musical instrument, and driving are only a few of the acts which the subconscious mind can be taught to do.

Driving is an excellent example of the usefulness of the subconscious mind. Has this ever happened to you? You drove home one night and never remembered any part of the trip! The subconscious mind took over and the conscious mind was free to do whatever it wanted to do. (This type of driving is risky to say the least, and certainly not recommended!)

Playing any kind of musical instrument demonstrates the most crucial difference between the conscious and subconscious minds. The conscious mind cannot do what the subconscious mind can do --- once the subconscious mind has learned. Some of the limitations of the conscious mind do not limit the subconscious mind. It is NOT possible to consciously play a piano the way Liberace plays. Only the subconscious mind could issue the commands to the muscles at the speed required to make the music of a Liberace.

Such human skills as playing the piano at the professional level can only be performed by letting the subconscious mind "do its own thing", by getting the conscious mind out of the way and letting it happen. How many times have you heard someone say, "His fingers have a mind of their own?" Well, now you know it's true.

The conscious mind is aware of the consequences of actions. It can sense fear, tension, anxiety, and can trigger some kind of bodily action. The subconscious does NOT think in terms of consequences; it thinks only in terms of performance in accordance with the way it has been taught.

It is obvious from the foregoing discussion that both the conscious and subconscious minds have roles to play in various types of human activity. The key to a sound mental game for bowling, and indeed for any sport, is to have each mind do its own thing, and not interfere with the actions of the other.

The conscious mind is very important in making several decisions while teaching the subconscious how to deliver the ball. The subconscious mind, once it has been taught correctly, has the responsibility to deliver the ball each time in exactly the manner it was taught. Thus, the conscious mind teaches and the subconscious mind acts.

The conscious mind is very important in making several decisions prior to the bowling session, and prior to each delivery: what ball to use; what line or angle seems to be the best for getting the ball into the pocket; what delivery adjustments, if any, need to be made; etc. And, if you are in a match, you might even want to give some conscious thought to your opposition.

These and other conscious thoughts all prepare you for the act of bowling. But, once these decisions have been made and you are on the approach, the subconscious mind needs to be set free of any interference from the conscious mind, free to deliver the ball in exactly the manner that it has been taught.

While the competition is underway, you need to continue making conscious decisions; evaluating what is happening and deciding what (if any) changes you need to make. A SOUND MENTAL GAME KEEPS BOTH MINDS WORKING IN HARMONY. However, it is the major responsibility of the subconscious mind to direct the muscles as they execute the approach and delivery.

The next section will take up the discussion of the conscious and subconscious minds, specifically addressing the need to develop subconscious competence. But, before going to that section, I would like to say a few words about the two characters who appear in the illustrations throughout this book.

I have created one character to represent MY CONscious mind, and named this character MYCON. The second character represents MY SUBconscious mind, and is appropriately named MYSUB. Both MYCON and MYSUB are used to illustrate aspects of the mental game which are explained in the various sections of the book.

MYCON is judgmental, can evaluate, can reason, is the thinker and the teacher, gives commands, learns things, can choose, and teaches the muscles. MYSUB is not-judgmental, can not evaluate, can not reason, is the student, is the doer, follows commands, stores what is learned, cannot choose, and directs the muscles to act.

MYCON appears in a solid black color, signifying something very visible. MYSUB is shaded to indicate something more in the background, as the subconscious mind is supposed to be.

Please take these illustrated messages seriously. I have tried to capture the essence of a significant part of the mental game in each illustration. I hope that putting the message in illustration form is an effective way of getting the message across, and that it makes reading this book a little more enjoyable.

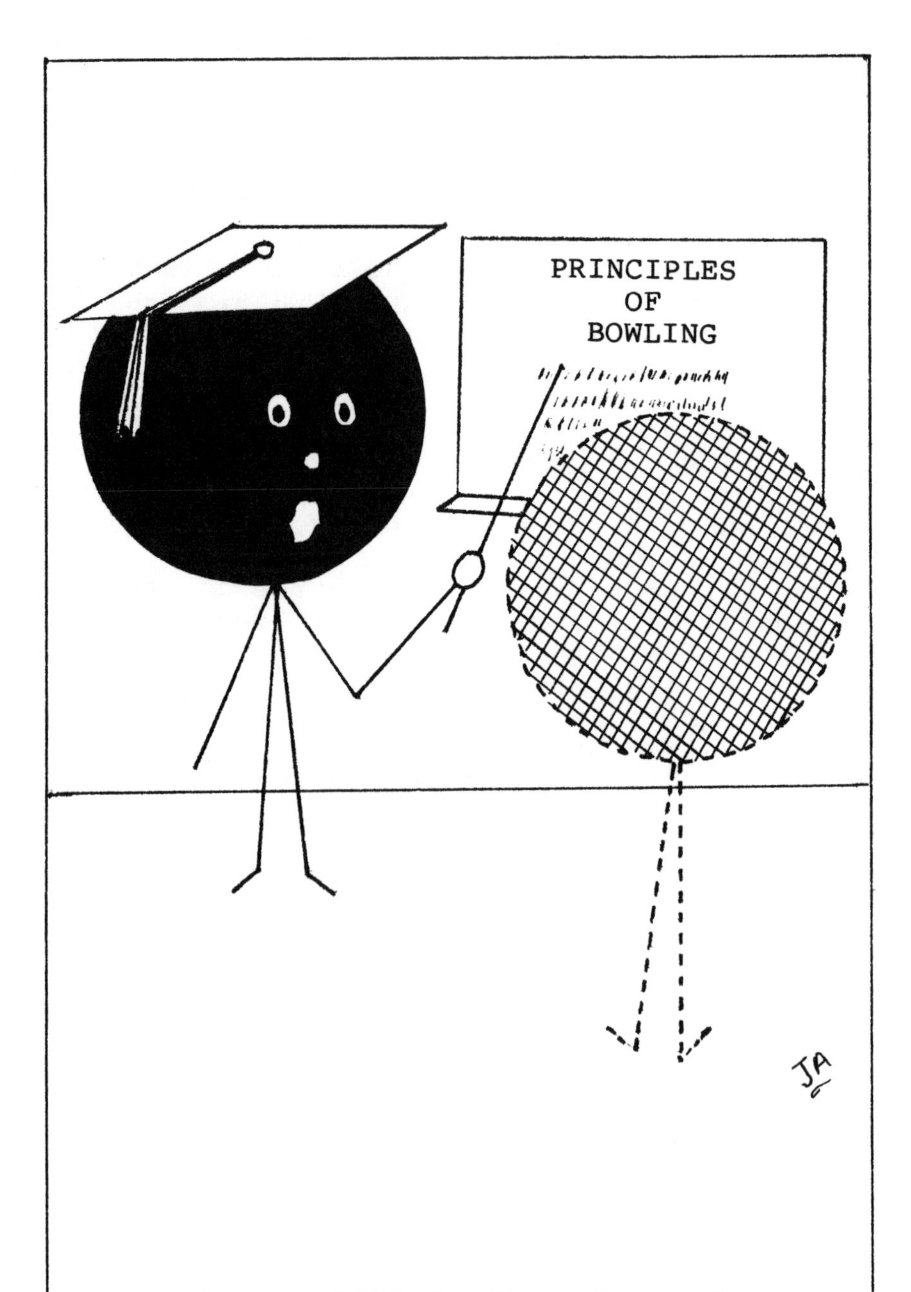

Every human skill is first learned under the critical guidance and supervision of the conscious mind.

--- THE GOAL OF ALL SKILL DEVELOPMENT EFFORTS IS SUBCONSCIOUS COMPETENCE. ---

As mentioned in Section 1, THE MENTAL GAME, there is both an inner and an outer game of bowling. The inner game is one which you play against yourself. The outer game is played against your opponent. The outcome of the inner struggle is far more significant in determining how much success you have on the lanes than the outer game played against your opponent. Your ability to fully utilize your mental game is the key to success in bowling.

The skill of an opponent in bowling cannot affect your personal performance, unless you let it affect you. Unlike the sport of tennis, for example, a strong opponent can affect your game, forcing you to run for the ball, come to the net, go to the back line, etc. With bowling, it is you and the ball and the pins. You are not in a head-to-head physical confrontation with an opponent when you bowl. You and the pins face each other, while your opponent is waiting to see what results you achieve.

How well you perform is a function of both your physical game and your mental game. Your physical game consists of your ability to deliver the ball in a consistent, natural and well-timed manner. Your mental game is far more complex, although the image most people have of bowling is the physical act of throwing the ball down the lane. In later sections I will address specific aspects of the mental game. Here we only wish to describe the concept of the "inner game", a term coined by Timothy Gallwey, and how it is played.

In Section 2, the discussion centered around the concept of conscious and subconscious minds. These are the two "opponents" in the inner game struggle. The relationship which exists between your conscious and subconscious minds is at the heart of the mental game. The goal is to develop a harmonious relationship, where each mind knows its own role, and one does not interfere with the other.

In "The Inner Game of Tennis", Timothy Gallwey refers to the conscious mind as Self 1 and the subconscious mind as Self 2. The conscious mind is, as described in the previous section, that portion of the mind which gives the instructions to the subconscious mind. The subconscious mind is responsible for performing the act for which it has been trained. The conscious mind tells the subconscious mind what to do. The subconscious mind will react without question to what it has been told to do. It does not make judgments; that is the province of the conscious mind.

Gallwey states that: "Within each player the kind of relationship that exists between Self 1 and Self 2 is the prime factor in determining one's ability to translate knowledge of technique into effective action... the key to better tennis --- or better anything ---lies in improving the relationship between the conscious teller, Self 1, and the unconscious, automatic doer, Self 2."

Instead of using the terms Self 1 and Self 2, we will continue to use the more descriptive terms conscious mind and subconscious mind, as described in the previous section. The inner game of bowling is a struggle between the thinking part of your mental game (the conscious mind) and the executing or doing part of it (the subconscious mind).

Essentially, the objective of the mental game (the game you have to play against yourself), is simply TO LET YOUR SUBCONSCIOUS MIND EXECUTE THE SHOT FREE FROM ANY INTERFERENCE FROM THE CONSCIOUS MIND. Though simple to state, such an objective is difficult to achieve. However, you can feel it when it happens. How often have you delivered the ball and KNEW as soon as it left your fingers that you had executed a perfect shot? Every part of the delivery felt effortless, natural, spontaneous, and free. You were certain you were going to make a strike or convert a spare, and you did.

During moments of perfect execution of the shot, there was no disharmony within your body. Your conscious mind was relaxed and trusted the subconscious mind to perform as it had been trained to perform. There was no fear of failure, nor was there any thought of failure. There was no conscious reminder to the subconscious mind of what had to be done. The subconscious mind was free to act in a spontaneous manner, as it directed the necessary muscles to deliver the ball.

Achieving such an inner harmony between the conscious and subconscious minds requires the development of certain mental skills, just as delivery of the ball requires the development of certain physical skills. ONCE THE DELIVERY BEGINS, IT IS NECESSARY TO DIVERT THE CONSCIOUS MIND SO THAT THE SUBCONSCIOUS CAN PERFORM WITHOUT INTERFERENCE. It is necessary to let the delivery happen, free from any judgment by the conscious mind as to how well the task is performed. It is necessary to develop trust in the ability of the muscles to perform in the spontaneous manner in which they have been trained.

Initially, both the conscious mind and subconscious mind are required to develop competence. Let's review these two aspects of the mental game to see how they provide insights into developing subconscious competence.

Skill development normally progresses through four distinct but related stages: (1) SUBCONSCIOUS INCOMPETENCE; (2) CONSCIOUS INCOMPETENCE; (3) CONSCIOUS COMPETENCE, and (4) SUBCONSCIOUS COMPETENCE. The fourth stage, subconscious competence, is the goal of all skill development.

Incidentally, this classification method is similar to many found in the literature on skill development, and has been adapted to this discussion on the development of the mental game of bowling. (The original author of this four-stage development cycle is unknown.) Sometimes the learning or relearning process is described as (1) unfreezing, (2) relearning, and (3) refreezing. I prefer, and will use the four stage process outlined above.

FIRST, there is the stage in which the person is not performing competently (is incompetent) but is not aware (is unconscious) of the fact that his actions are incorrect. At this point in the skill development cycle, we say the person is SUBCONSCIOUSLY INCOMPETENT. With no instruction or no attempt to learn correct technique, minimum skill will be developed. The person may improve slightly, but may also deeply ingrain bad habits (train the subconscious incorrectly) which may be either difficult or impossible to change at a later time.

The SECOND stage in skill development occurs when the person becomes aware of what actions they are performing (they are conscious of these actions), even though they may not be able to correct their mistakes. They are still performing their actions incorrectly (they are still incompetent) but now they are aware of what they are doing. This stage in the skill development cycle is called the CONSCIOUS INCOMPETENCE phase. An awareness of the fact that you are performing incorrectly is the first step in skill development. Admitting that your actions are incorrect is the next required step, or else no corrective actions will occur. This stage does not last very long if the person wants to improve.

The THIRD stage really begins the skill development. The person begins to show signs of properly executing the actions needed to deliver the ball properly (he is somewhat competent), but these correct motions (the delivery) take deliberate, conscious effort to achieve some measure of success. This third stage in the development cycle is referred to as CONSCIOUS COMPETENCE. The person has not reached his maximum performance level, but he is more competent then he was, and is still improving. However, he must consciously think of what he has to do while he is doing it.

The FOURTH or final stage in skill development occurs when performance is executed correctly (competently) and the person appears to do everything naturally and freely, without any conscious thoughts (subconsciously). At this skill level, the subconscious mind is permitted to execute and control delivery of the ball, with no interference from the conscious mind telling it what to do. The person does not have to think about what is happening, he just lets it happen. The bowler has reached the fourth, or SUBCONSCIOUS COMPETENCE, stage of skill development.

When you have reached the fourth level of skill development, your movements and actions in the delivery should be as automatic as the movements of the fingers of a skilled pianist. It is impossible for the conscious mind to direct the fingers to play a piano well (or any musical instrument for that matter). Only the sub-conscious mind could control such movements. It is impossible to directly control the fingers when typing 100 words per minute. The subconscious mind controls and directs the fingers. It is not possible to directly and consciously control the movement of the feet when you are dancing well. The music sends signals to the subconscious mind which directs the feet to the beat of the music. These are only a few related examples of actions and movements of the body which are controlled by the subconscious mind, and which illustrate the LIMITATIONS of the conscious mind.

Your approach and delivery should be developed to such a state that you need give it no conscious thought whatsoever. It just happens. At that point you have developed subconscious competence. You have trained your subconscious mind to take control, to direct your feet in the steps, and your arm in the swing as automatically as if you were walking. (Walking is yet another example of subconscious competence. Observe a few deliberate, conscious steps of a toddler learning to walk. Then watch the same child once it has mastered the art of walking.)

Once you have developed automatic mental and muscular patterns of action (through proper conscious practice), they can occur naturally (subconsciously) if you will let them happen. The conscious mind can and must be distracted --- and let the subconscious mind perform.

In golf, this distraction of the conscious mind occurs by "keeping your eyes on the ball". In bowling, this distraction occurs by "keeping your eyes on your target on the lane". One of the major benefits from using a targeting system for aiming is the ability to distract your conscious mind during the delivery.

Your conscious thoughts should occur before you take your stance, and end when the pushaway begins. The subconscious mind takes over from the pushaway until the follow-through is completed. The conscious mind comes back into play after the ball passes over the target, so you can determine what conscious adjustments you may have to make should the shot not result in a strike or spare.

An "instinctive bowler" illustrates an excellent example of how the subconscious mind works. Such a bowler is able to sense that he has made some small mistake in his delivery, and will automatically make an adjustment to correct the error.

To conclude, the conscious mind cannot do, on a consistent basis, what the subconscious mind has been trained to do. Now you can see why pressure shots are often bad shots. The bowler's conscious mind tells his subconscious mind that "this shot is too important to trust to you." The conscious mind (MYCON) says, "I'll make this shot myself". Inevitably, the shot is bad, usually high on the head pin because the conscious mind "made sure" of the shot. Billy Welu was correct: "Trust is a must or your game is a bust". You must learn to trust your subconscious.

The sections which follow will discuss many factors which have a direct and indirect bearing on your ability to develop an inner harmony between the conscious and subconscious mind. When you are able to execute all your shots (deliver the ball) in a subconscious, spontaneous and relaxed manner, free from the interference of the conscious mind, then you will have mastered a very large portion of the mental game, the inner game of bowling.

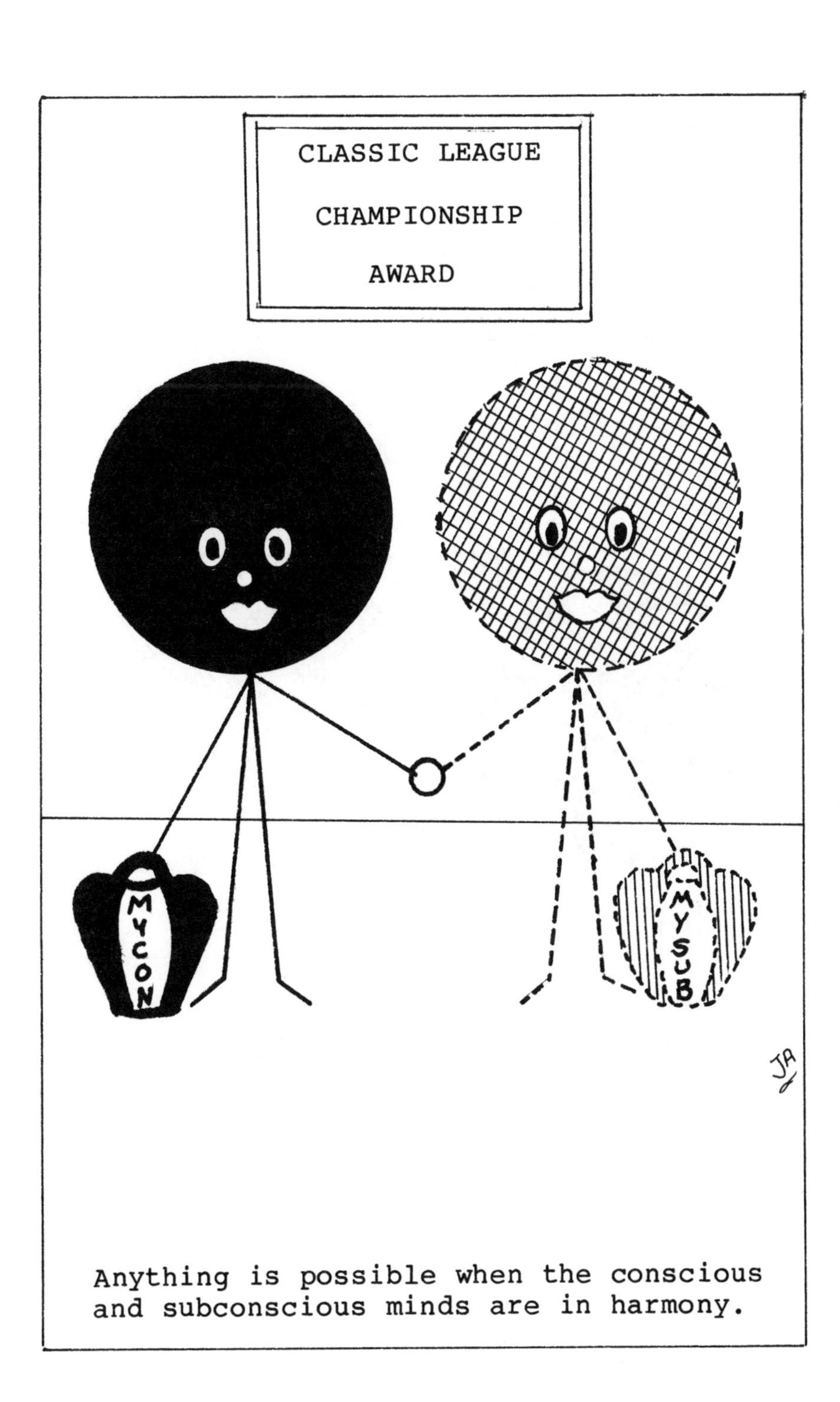

Anything is possible when the conscious and subconscious minds are in harmony.

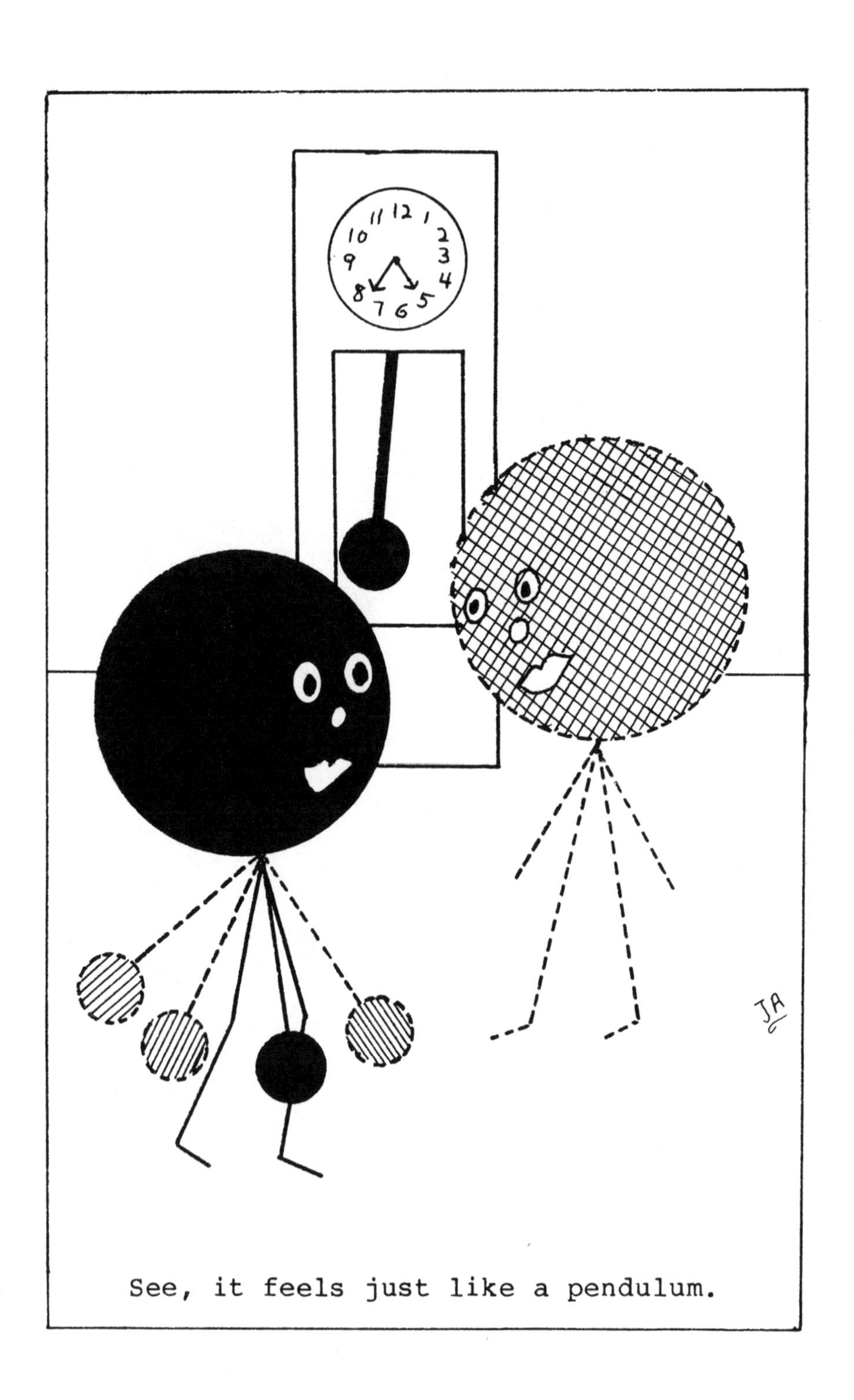

See, it feels just like a pendulum.

--- YOUR AWARENESS OF YOUR ACTIONS IN THE APPROACH AND DELIVERY BECOMES THE STANDARD BY WHICH YOU ASSESS YOUR PERFORMANCE ---

Sensitivity is a heightened awareness of what is happening, while it is happening. This awareness is strengthened by your knowledge of the activity. For example, your knowledge of the fundamentals of bowling and your game in particular, can make you very sensitive and aware of what is happening when you deliver the ball.

A skilled person in any field is more alert, more aware, more sensitive to events which are not obvious to the untrained person. A skilled auto mechanic can detect the slightest change in the sound of the motor, and may even be able to diagnose trouble before it occurs. A skilled artist can detect minute flaws in art that would probably never be seen by the unskilled viewer. An airline pilot is very attuned to the sound of the engines and would notice the slightest sound that was not normal. A skilled bowler can detect tiny flaws in the delivery as they occur. These heightened sensitivities are the result of skill development.

Skill development means acquiring the right feelings or sensitivities in many areas. Good bowling is a game of sensing and feeling. When you are bowling well, you feel a certain way. When you are bowling poorly, the good feeling is not there. All the required motions for delivering the ball are subject to being sensed, and can be sensed by the high-average bowler.

Initially, you should consciously try to develop in your mind and body, a total feeling of what happens when you are bowling well. Your total feeling of bowling well centers upon your feelings while you are in the stance, and during each movement from the pushaway until you have completed the follow through.

Inherent in this feeling is the use of the proper principles, fundamentals, or basics. What does it feel like when you are executing each shot perfectly? Remember these feelings so you have the standard by which you can judge your performance. If the feelings are correct, you are executing your shots well. If the feelings are not correct, you are making a mistake in your delivery. You want to be able to sense this deviation from the feelings you have when you are executing the delivery properly. Then you are in a position to locate these mistakes and correct them. What you have developed is a method for self-analysis that can lead to self-development.

This feeling is sometimes referred to as a TOTAL STRIKE FEELING, although the delivery for the strike and spare should be basically the same. The motions for the stance, pushaway, swing, steps, slide, release, balance position, and follow through should not change. Therefore, these feelings, when you are rolling your strike ball perfectly, are what we are talking about. What does it feel like when you are bowling well?

Has this happened to you? You release the ball in a normal manner. You see it on the lane, and previous experiences tell you almost immediately that you have rolled the ball well. You know in advance that it is going to be a strike, or at least a solid pocket hit. Very often it is a strike. You had that strike feeling.

It is this feeling that you have executed the shot perfectly that you want to remember, the feeling that you executed all parts of the delivery exactly as planned. The delivery felt perfect.

You don't relate to these feelings until you see the ball on that portion of the lane which has given you success before. Now, come back to the approach in your thoughts. Don't think of anything beyond the arrows. From your stance position to your finish at the foul line, feel, absorb, and think of how you felt when you did everything exactly correct. Concentrate on these feelings. Your subconscious mind should be trying to repeat these feelings, to duplicate them on each delivery, with no conscious thought on your part. Let the sub-conscious mind remember and repeat the correct movements which create the right feelings.

If you can capture these feelings, can sense when the movements are correct, you have an excellent chance to groove a consistent, natural and well-timed delivery that you can repeat time and time again. To illustrate this concept, let's discuss three specific feelings, and show you how to put these feelings into use in all your deliveries.

These three feelings of bowling you should develop are: (1) the feeling of lift, (2) the shoulder-up feeling , and (3) the feeling of the true pendulum swing. Awareness and sensitivity to these three parts of the delivery will provide you with the basis by which you can develop awareness of other motions in the delivery.

Lift is the spin imparted on the ball at the moment it is released off the tips of the fingers. What does lift feel like?

How do you achieve a true feeling of lift? To illustrate, stand with your bowling arm hanging down by your side. Take your two bowling fingers and bend them inward toward the palm of the hand, as though they were inserted in the ball. Take the index finger of your other hand and roll it off the closed fingers, similar to the ball rolling off them at the release point. Hold the two bowling fingers in the bent position. Do not let them straighten out. These fingers continue to have an inward, bent pressure, as your other index finger rolls off them. The true feeling of lift comes from the fingers trying to stay in the bent position, similar to a coil which returns to its prior shape after you straighten it. It recoils; it returns to its normally coiled position. Try to isolate and remember this feeling of lift so that you can be aware of it while it is happening in the delivery.

The shoulder-up feeling is the second area for developing a sense of feel. If your shoulder is pointed downward in a lazy manner, is not held upward in a strong position, your arm can swing in a number of directions: left, right, behind the back, away from the body, etc. There are many opportunities for the swing to be incorrect, to deviate from the straight swing. You tend to lose accuracy. The feeling of a pendulum swing is difficult to achieve when the shoulder is down. There is a tendency to guide the ball, to pull it or to muscle it. You tend to help the ball rather than let the ball swing in a natural manner.

Put the shoulder down. Put the arm back behind the body; move the arm out to the side, away from the body, behind the back, forward, to the right, left, everywhere. The arm is very flexible when the shoulder is down. It goes in every direction. If that were the swing with the ball, the ball might go in any direction.

Now, stand with the right shoulder raised slightly, perhaps no more than a half of an inch. (Raise your left shoulder if you are left handed.) Take you arm back, and try to put your arm behind your body WITHOUT bending your elbow. It will not go behind your body when the shoulder is held in this up position. Sideways motion of the arm is restricted when the shoulder is positioned in this manner, and a straight swing should occur.

Now, swing your arm forward and backward as though your were making your normal swing. It is very difficult to pull the arm to the left or right as long as the shoulder is in this slightly raised position. A true pendulum or straight swing is more likely. The shoulder becomes the hinge-point for the pendulum swing.

The rhythm of the pendulum swing is an even motion, with the same speed occurring throughout the swing. There is no effort exerted at any point in the swing. The speed of the swing is determined by the weight of the ball. This results in a true pendulum swing feeling. The ball is not working against the arm, and the arm is not trying to force the ball. The ball will seem very light if the rhythm of the swing is correct.

Try swinging the ball gently by your side, letting the weight of the ball determine the speed and arc of the swing. That is the feeling of the pendulum swing that you should be sensing as you bowl.

These three feelings are the first ones you should develop in your overall strike feeling: the feeling of lift; the shoulder-up feeling; and the true pendulum swing feeling. Let these feelings become so natural that any deviation from them when you are bowling will become immediately noticeable.

Of course the delivery is composed of more motions than these three. Skill development in bowling requires that you develop a set of motions and movements which are as close to mechanical perfection as possible. Even though you try to do exactly the same thing each time you roll the ball, you cannot become an automatic, robot-like bowler. Some small differences will occur simply because you are human, and you want to become sensitive and aware of these minute, unintended changes.

If you can develop a delivery that is composed of the correct motions (for you), and can SUBCONSCIOUSLY repeat these motions time and time again, then you will have achieved the degree of consistency that is necessary to master the delivery. At the same time, you must take into consideration your physical and mental characteristics, as well as your personality and temperament. The motions in your approach and delivery should be tailor-made to suit you, yet follow the principles of good bowling.

The more perfectly you have developed the motions in the delivery, the more precise you can be in all of your deliveries. The more consistent you are, the more you will roll high scores on a regular basis, and the less you will have to rely upon luck or lane conditions to help your scoring and average.

Try to perfect the motions of your delivery to as close to machine-like precision as you are capable of achieving: the same stance posture, the same pushaway, the same rhythm and tempo to your steps, the same straight pendulum-like swing, the same slide and release, and the same good follow through. This consistency of performance will become your standard for detecting any changes that might occur.

Every movement of your body and the ball should be pre-determined and have a specific purpose. No motion should occur unless it is necessary for a perfect delivery. Each motion you make is something you have to master; something you have to do correctly; and something you have to subconsciously remember. Obviously, the less motions you have in your delivery, the fewer things you will have to do correctly to execute the shot well.

What motions are required? You must take some number of steps toward the foul line, and you must swing the ball and release it toward the pins. Coordinate these two actions, the steps and the swing, so they are as effortless and natural as possible. Develop them to the point that you can repeat them in a consistent manner over a long period of time. Reduce the number of motions and you reduce the possibility for errors.

One possible exception is a movement or action that helps you relax or get set for the approach. You may make some small movement of the ball during the stance TO RELAX YOURSELF. If the movement or action does not interfere with a good delivery, then it may not need to be eliminated. That is the key point. Does the motion contribute to a good delivery, or does it detract from the delivery?

Keep in mind that the delivery is one smooth, continuous, fluid motion. This motion begins with the pushaway and ends with the follow through.

Initially you will have to concentrate on each motion or action in the delivery. Later, this conscious thought process will have to be replaced by an almost automatic, subconscious performance. You will not have to consciously think about the correct actions once they are mastered, nor can you think about them as they occur during the delivery. They will have to occur automatically, with no conscious thought on your part. When you have achieved that level of subconscious competence you will have perfected a good delivery, and now have the potential for achieving a high average. Other aspects of the conscious and subconscious mental game will still have to be developed.

Develop your own individual style of movements from the stance to the foul line, centered around your physical build, mental outlook and temperament. Principles of the physical game allow you to capitalize on your physical assets and minimize your physical weaknesses as they relate to bowling. Principles of the mental game allow you to develop a strong mental game. Let your delivery reflect your physical and mental characteristics.

Develop a delivery composed of relaxed and effortless actions, a delivery that puts little or no strain on your wrist, fingers, arm or body. Such a style of bowling is one that can be used for many years. I have previously mentioned that bowling is a game of relaxed muscles. Let your delivery be as relaxed and effortless as possible.

Develop a set of feelings which are comfortable to you when you are executing the approach and delivery properly. Your sensitivity to and awareness of these feelings ideally will become the basis by which you judge your performance. When the feelings are correct, you should be bowling well. When the feelings are not correct, you will have the basis for deciding what you are doing incorrectly.

A natural feeling or motion for one person may not feel natural for another.

That is why you must find out what motions feel natural to you when you are bowling well, and incorporate these actions into your delivery. This also explains why a certain motion or action may work well for one bowler but not for another.

Develop all parts of your approach and delivery to such a consistent level that you can repeat each motion, each movement, with almost no conscious thought on your part. Your subconscious mind must eventually take over all details of the approach and delivery. If you have to consciously think about what you have to do, you may NOT be able to do these things properly. Knowledge of this fact is sometimes used to try psyching-out an opponent. (See Section 12, PSYCHING YOUR OPPONENT OUT.)

The more firmly you can incorporate approach and delivery movements into your subconscious mind, the more you should be able to repeat these actions over and over again in exactly the same manner. It is this level of subconscious repetitiveness, this degree of consistency, which assures you of little deviation from delivery to delivery. Subconscious or second nature actions get the muscles to work together, producing little or no strain.

In conclusion, it is necessary to develop an awareness and sensitivity to all parts of the approach and delivery. Each motion must be incorporated into a subconscious pattern of action that allows you to execute the delivery in exactly the same manner each frame of each game. Your approach and delivery must occur subconsciously, with the conscious mind not interfering with it at all.

You must reduce the number and type of motions in your approach and delivery to the barest essentials, only doing what you feel is necessary to deliver the ball properly.

This will initially take conscious thoughts, but will eventually lead to subconscious actions once you have started your approach. Then, if you make any planned or unplanned deviation from your normal approach and delivery, you will know what you have done differently, and be in a position to take corrective action.

Your awareness of all parts of the approach and delivery becomes the standard by which you can constantly assess what you are doing. That is the goal or objective of heightened sensitivity and awareness.

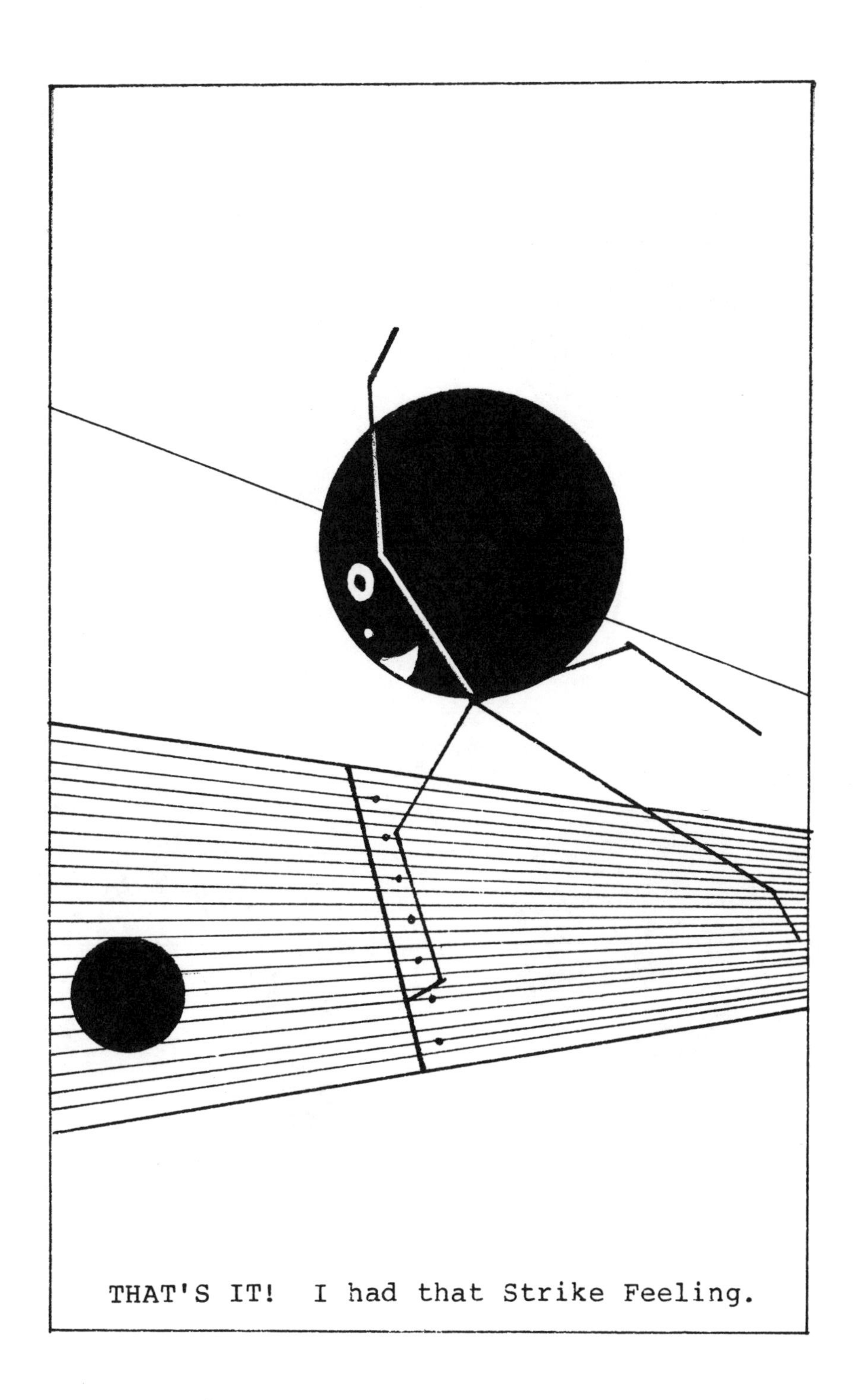
THAT'S IT! I had that Strike Feeling.

ELBOW TUCKED?
EYES ON TARGET?
DON'T DRIFT!
Blah..Blah
...Mffff...
Mffff...
JA

--- WHEN YOU DO SOMETHING NATURALLY, YOU DO NOTHING AT ALL. YOU JUST LET IT HAPPEN. ---

When a skillful bowler is executing his or her shots perfectly, it looks so effortless and natural. Spectators often cannot appreciate what skills are needed to perform so well. This is true in any sport. The higher the skill level, the less effort the performance seems to require. All actions seem natural for the performer, and in fact they usually are.

What is natural for you (height of backswing, speed and number of steps, speed and arc of the swing, etc.) will seem effortless. What is not natural for you will require effort and create muscle strain. What you should develop is a delivery pattern you can rely upon to perform the same body and ball motions time and time again, in an automatic, spontaneous, subconscious, robot-like fashion. This is often referred to as a GROOVED DELIVERY. To bowl well, consistently, requires such a delivery.

The development of a natural delivery has three requirements: (1) let your natural body motions make up the major portion of the delivery; (2) develop a subconscious delivery, in line with the previous section on developing subconscious competence, and (3) let your delivery style agree with your attitude, temperament, and personality. An effective approach and delivery will appear to be automatic responses and actions, triggered by the conscious mind, but requiring little or no conscious thought. All parts of the approach and delivery will occur in a free-flowing manner.

In effect, you should train your entire body to bowl as naturally as you walk up a flight of stairs, which requires no conscious effort once it has been learned. However, try walking up a flight of stairs and CONSCIOUSLY give your legs these instructions. You may find that each step is a deliberate effort if it is done consciously, yet requires no effort when delegated to the subconscious mind. Once you have learned how to walk up a flight of stairs, it occurs naturally.

What we consider to be NATURAL body motions are actually ACQUIRED in most cases. What we practice eventually will feel very comfortable to us; it feels natural. What we have learned becomes a part of us.

If you practice anything long enough it will become a natural part of all your actions and movements. Thus, naturalness is learned behavior, and not traits or skills acquired at birth. This explains why any change in your approach or delivery feels uncomfortable (unnatural) at first. It also explains why you may bowl poorly while you are practicing a delivery change.

It is just as easy to execute the delivery correctly as it is to do it incorrectly. In fact, it should be easier to do it correctly, if you take advantage of your natural talents. It is just as natural to make incorrect motions as it is to make correct ones. This means that what you learn you consider natural for you. If you have learned incorrect motions as part of your delivery, you must unlearn them and learn the correct ones. These new patterns of movement will then seem natural to you.

The above comments indicate why incorrect practice can actually hinder your performance instead of helping it. Poor practice is often worse than no practice at all. If you practice the wrong actions, these incorrect movements will seem natural to you. They only feel natural because you have practiced them. Then, when you want to learn the correct way (another way) you must rid yourself of the previously learned patterns, and develop new and different ones. This means that muscles which have been developed to perform in a certain manner, must be re-taught new patterns of movement.

When you do something naturally, in effect you do not do anything at all. You simply let it happen. For example, if you let the ball swing in a free-flowing or pendulum manner, with no conscious effort on your part, then this action can be said to just happen. It does itself. You do not force it to occur, you exert no effort. In effect, you get out of the way and let it happen, naturally.

The release illustrates another part of the delivery where you should let it happen. Do not grip the ball and open your hand to release it. LET THE BALL RELEASE ITSELF; let it come off the fingers and thumb naturally. Let the release happen.

Such natural movements and actions can be repeated time and time again in exactly the same manner. Natural actions should lead to consistent and well-timed deliveries.

Here is another example of a natural action which may affect how you bowl. Stand with both feet together. Now take three or four steps. Do this several times. Which foot did you start with each time? One foot will seem more natural for starting than the other. If you naturally start with the left foot, you might consider using the 5-step approach, which begins with the left foot. (A left hander would use the 4-step approach.) If you naturally start with the right foot, then the 4-step approach might be more comfortable (natural) for you. (A left hander would use the 5-step approach.)

Forcing things to happen, instead of letting them happen, makes it more difficult to get them to occur in a consistent manner. Any time you interfere with natural movements, either to do something or refrain from doing something, you have to exert effort. This creates the possibility for mistakes, and is often the source of fatigue. If the action or movement happens naturally, it will normally happen exactly the same way each time, and require less effort. If you must consciously make the action happen, you force it to occur, it is far more likely that you will not be able to repeat the motion or action exactly the same way each time. The most effective deliveries are those which are the result of natural body actions and are relatively free of effort. Such deliveries are more likely to be consistent and well-timed.

Unnatural is a word which is similar in concept to forced. An action that does not seem natural for you has to be forced upon your body. Try running at full speed. That is not natural and will take force, both mental and physical, to keep yourself running. Walking, on the other hand, is more natural to adults (those without physical handicaps). It takes very little physical effort to walk for long distances, and takes virtually no mental effort. It has become a subconscious, natural process.

It is more difficult to repeat forced actions than it is to repeat natural ones. It takes conscious effort and thought to do anything that is not natural. There is no tension, strain or anxiety associated with natural actions. Natural actions are relaxed actions, and bowling is an activity that is performed best with relaxed muscles. Therefore, the more you can perfect your delivery to the point that all parts of it just happen naturally, the greater will be your potential for bowling well over a long period of time.

If you rely upon physical strength and mental effort to force all actions in the delivery, then you are going to have to make major adjustments as you age. If you can rely upon natural timing, rhythm, and coordination (an easy and relaxed delivery), you will have to make less changes as you get older. You will still have to make some changes, but they should be gradual and minor.

Fatigue, both mental and physical, may occur with the use of effort. Fatigue makes it difficult to maintain consistency, and creates errors and delivery faults. The more effort you expend in your delivery the more you will have to contend with fatigue. This is another argument in favor of an effortless, tension-free delivery, one that is natural. The less effort you require as a normal part of your delivery, the less you will have to change as your energy level falls, either during a long bowling session, or as a consequence of the aging process. An effortless and natural delivery will minimize fatigue, allowing you to bowl more lines per session, and more sessions. It is the type of delivery that will let you bowl well for as many years as you care to do so, and which requires the least amount of change and adjustment as you age.

Fatigue is definitely a major factor in tournament bowling, especially at the professional level where it may be necessary to bowl up to 16 games in a single day. Six and eight game blocks per day are normal in such events. Bowling 42 to 56 games for the week is also normal. Any action which reduces mental or physical fatigue to manageable levels must necessarily be beneficial for your game. NATURAL MOTIONS REDUCE FATIGUE.

Comfort is another word associated with naturalness. Being natural means being comfortable and relaxed. If a particular action feels comfortable to you, try to incorporate it into your approach or delivery. For example, if you feel comfortable starting on your left foot, yet you want to use a 4-step approach, you can do that. Take one step with your left foot and do not move the ball. Then, on your second step move the ball out into the pushaway as suggested in the 4-step delivery. In effect, you will have a 5-step approach and a 4-step delivery. (Left handers would start with the right foot.)

If you feel uncomfortable not moving the ball for the first step, and want to move the ball at the same time you take the first step, this can also be incorporated into your delivery. Hold the ball slightly away from your body and bring it back toward you as you take your first step. Then push it away at the beginning of the second step.

These two examples illustrate how it is possible to incorporate into your delivery those motions which are comfortable for you. Make your approach and delivery as comfortable as possible, and these natural actions will go a long way toward the development of a consistent and well-timed delivery.

There is an element of truth in the statement that the personality of a bowler is often reflected in the manner in which he or she bowls. The delivery style is often in harmony with the personality.

Two distinct types of deliveries characterize most high-average bowlers. These two styles are called STROKER (classic) and CRANKER (power step) deliveries. The style that is most comfortable and natural for you may be dependent upon your personality or other mental factors. The following is a brief summary of these bowling styles.

The CLASSIC style might be considered the more natural of the two. The ball will determine the speed of the swing, which then determines the pace of the steps. Almost no force is used in the approach and delivery.

The steps are taken in a smooth, effortless manner. The slide coincides with the arrival of the ball at the foul line, and the ball is released in a firm yet relaxed manner. There is very little twisting or spinning of the ball, and a more or less straight angle is used on the strike delivery, using a normal hook ball pattern. Natural timing, coordination, rhythm, pace, and tempo are key elements in the classic-type delivery.

The CRANKER style is one in which the swing is more controlled or forced. The cranker decides where the ball is located at any point during the delivery, and forces or deliberately sets the pace of the swing. The ball is muscled far more than in the stroker delivery. The cranker plants the sliding foot at the foul line while the ball is still coming forward but is not beside the foot. An effort is exerted to put fingers, spin, turn, action, etc. on the ball at the moment it is released. An open foul line angle is often used with the cranker-type delivery, although all five strike lines are used at one time or another.

The cranker gets under the ball, keeps the arm close to the body, and uses more wrist action (lift and turn) than the stroker. The cranker also aims for an area, instead of having a specific board as a target. The cranker is also noted for carrying light-pocket or half-pocket hits. The cranker needs excellent balance to get the proper amount of leverage into the shot.

Power bowlers often have trouble with their spares. They tend to be less accurate than strokers, and accuracy is far more important on some spares than on strikes. Power bowlers, crankers, often try to overpower the lanes. Strokers try to play the lane, to adapt to the lane instead of trying to overpower it.

Whether a bowler prefers the stroker or cranker style is in some measure dependent upon personality, level of aggression, competitive nature, and other personality factors. The more aggressive individual may decide upon the cranker style, while a more easy-going, relaxed, person might select the stroker method.

Physical factors are also important. Less effort is required for the stroker type delivery, making it easier to execute over a long period of time. If you are physically strong you may prefer the cranker delivery.

Neither style is necessarily any better than the other. Both are good styles. But, each person will naturally tend toward one or the other.

Determine your natural style as soon as you can and begin developing it. Watch those who bowl with a similar style. Try to incorporate into your delivery all the best features of those deliveries you find most effective, but which are also consistent with your preferences, natural talents, abilities and temperament.

Observe the natural styles of some of the more successful bowlers. Notice the wide range of individual characteristics they display. Yet we can say that their delivery style is natural for them. And, that is the important point. You do not need to become a carbon copy of anyone else; you should be you. Develop a delivery that is natural for you.

If your natural delivery allows you to achieve a high average, to score well on a consistent basis, then whatever you are doing is correct. You must determine what type of delivery works well for you, that feels natural and comfortable, and develop your delivery along those natural lines.

Luck is a major factor in bowling.

--- YOU CAN'T CONTROL LUCK, BUT YOU CAN CONTROL ITS IMPACT UPON YOU. ---

Bowling is one of the few sports in which you can make one or more mistakes in performance, and yet achieve perfection in the frame: a strike. In fact, it is possible to do almost everything INcorrectly and yet score a strike. This often happens to beginners.

It is possible to hit the head pin very light, very heavy, on the brooklyn side, or not at all, and still score a strike. And there is no way to totally remove this luck aspect from the game. In fact, if you could, bowling would probably lose some of its attraction for many bowlers.

Therefore, we must conclude that the luck factor is something every serious bowler is going to have to contend with, and must develop a mental attitude that lets luck contribute to his game but not detract from it.

Luck may be good or bad. It is good when it favors you or disfavors your opponents. It is bad when it favors them or disfavors you. Thus, what happens does not determine whether luck is good or bad, it all depends upon who it favors or disfavors.

The inevitability of luck as an integral part of the game of bowling should allow you to accept it as just another condition you have to contend with, and not become overly concerned about it. You should only concern yourself with things over which you have some control. And, you have no real control over luck. Since you cannot change it, and you cannot get rid of it, do not let luck affect your game. Face it philosophically; accept it and forget it.

It is only when you become distressed about it, that luck can interfere with your performance. Therefore, this puts you in the position to minimize the detrimental impact luck has on your mental game. You can decide to accept it as it happens and not react in any manner. Or you can decide to become upset when luck favors your opponents. It is your decision to make.

An ATTITUDE OF ACCEPTANCE will go a long way toward reducing the impact of luck on your game. In effect, you are not controlling luck, but you are CONTROLLING ITS IMPACT upon you. Besides, in the long run, luck should even itself out, favoring you as often as it disfavors you.

Before looking at ways to develop an attitude of acceptance toward luck, I would like to review the change in the luck factor as it relates to bowling, especially since the early 1960's.

The luck factor in bowling is far more dominant now than it used to be. Prior to about the year 1961, you had to hit the pocket, from the proper angle, at the correct speed, and with the right amount of action on the ball to strike. Currently, none of these four factors is essential to strike on a regular and consistent basis. Now, it is not even necessary to hit the pocket to strike on a fairly consistent basis.

A light, thin hit on the head pin often sends that pin off the kickback and onto the pin deck. The head pin often takes out the 2, 4, 5, 7, 8 and 10 pins by itself! These thin hits, mixers, wall shots, etc., are perhaps more responsible for high scores

--- without skill --- than any other factor in bowling, including blocked lanes. Thus, you have to be both lucky and skillful to score well in bowling, but luck is sometimes more important than skill.

At a bowling tournament in Las Vegas in 1983, almost 60% of the strikes were made on non-pocket hits! This is an incredible statistic. It means that luck played a bigger role than skill in many games. This was particularly true in the final or championship game. One team bowled better, in terms of hitting the pocket, but the other team carried more lucky (non-pocket) strikes. In fact, the game was won when the 6 pin bounced out of the pit and took out the 7-pin, on the very difficult 6-7-10 split. (The Championship game of the 1983 American Dream Classic, worth $250,000, was won when two "lucky strikes" fell.)

SKILL and LUCK can be placed on opposite ends of a continuum (a line), as shown below. One end represents pure skill, and the other end represents pure luck.

A RECREATION and a SPORT can also be placed at opposite ends of the same line or continuum. Skill is required in a sporting activity, but luck is more prevalent in a recreational activity.

```
PURE LUCK                                PURE SKILL
---------------------------------------------------
RECREATION                                    SPORT
```

It appears that the skill requirement for scoring well has been reduced in order to attract and retain recreational bowlers: women and children; mixed leagues; and the non-serious league bowler (often referred to as a "beer bowler"). In fact, the major transition in bowling since the early 1960's has been from bowling as a competitive sport to bowling as a recreational activity.

The apparent price for the growth and development of bowling as a recreational activity --- as a COMMERCIAL activity --- has been a general reduction in the skill required to score well. Luck has become a dominant factor in scoring, negating some of the skill requirements. Bowling has shifted from an activity that requires pure skill (a sport) to one that's dominated by luck (a recreation).

Double-voided pins, highly resilient kickbacks, phenolic pin decks, light pins, lane blocking, balls that almost hook by themselves (so-called exotic bowling balls), etc., have all combined to lessen the skill required to score well ON A CONSISTENT BASIS. Far too many games and tournaments are won by the person who was luckier than the one who hit the pocket consistently. (In many cases, the environment of bowling currently rewards non-pocket hits and penalizes pocket hits!) The dominant role of the luck factor is the single item which may prevent bowling from taking its proper place as a true sport.

It is not the purpose of this book to call for a return to skill requirements, nor to lessen the effect of luck on scoring. It is my purpose to point out that luck is such a dominant factor that your mental game has to be expanded to include the proper attitude toward luck.

You have to learn how to cope with luck, to accept good luck for your opponents and bad luck for yourself. (It is easy to accept BAD luck for your OPPONENTS, and GOOD luck for YOURSELF.) Lets look at some ways you can cope with the luck factor.

"Attitudes are more important than facts.", according to Norman Vincent Peale, a noted author on positive thinking. Thus, your attitude towards good and bad luck, particularly bad luck, is very important to your mental game.

You must learn how to accept defeat even when you have bowled better (hit the pocket more) than your opponent. This is a difficult mental attitude to develop, but it is very necessary to your overall mental game. Until skill requirements are returned to bowling, luck will play a MAJOR role in deciding who will win or lose, and you have to learn to accept this situation.

Some bowlers have the "mental fault" of getting upset when luck favors their opponent. They get upset and tense when their opponent gets what they consider a lucky break (a wall-shot strike, brooklyn, a "cave-in strike", etc.). When you get upset it tends to have a detrimental impact on your game. You become tense, your muscles tighten, your mental game erodes, you become unable to deliver the ball in your normal, subconscious, relaxed manner.

To overcome this problem, some people will never watch their opponents bowl, thus they never see their opposition get a lucky break, and it can have no effect upon their mental game. Professional bowler Frank Ellenberg has stated, "If you don't see your opponent get a luck break, it can't affect you psychologically." This tactic can be very useful if you are the type of person who gets upset with the good luck of your opponents.

Another way to mentally contend with luck is to keep in mind that bowling is a game in which there is no defense. There is nothing morally or legally that you can do to prevent your opponent from scoring well. (Well, not exactly. Section 12 explores the various methods used at times in attempts to PSYCH-OUT opponents.) The only thing you can do is bowl as well as you can and hope your score is high enough to win. Concentrate totally on your own game and ignore what your opponent is doing.

Don't complain about your bad luck on the lanes, and don't brag about your good luck. Take both as they come. Bowlers have a tendency to attribute high scores to good execution and poor scores to bad luck or bad conditions. Don't use luck as an alibi. Luck, skill and conditions are all part of the game. Don't let your good luck deceive you into thinking that your performance is better than it is. Don't rely upon luck. Develop skill that you can count on each time, and accept responsibility for your performances, both good and bad.

Sometimes you are going to hit the pocket in what you consider an absolutely perfect manner. Yet a pin or pins will remain standing, usually the 8 or 9 pin, or the 7 or 10 pin. Sometimes you will leave the 7-10 split on what looks like a perfect pocket hit. This can be distressing, but need not be. Why not SALUTE THE STANDING PINS? Salute them, acknowledging them as very worthy opponents who have stood up against your best shot. Or, do as Toby Contreras might do; SMILE AT THEM.

This is difficult to do, particularly at a crucial time in a match. However, you cannot change what has happened, only your reaction to it. Bad thoughts can harm your performance; good thoughts will generally help performance. Therefore, why let something that you can do nothing about, cause you problems in future frames and games? Why not use those opportunities to develop your mental game? You will benefit if you do, and probably pay the price if you don't.

It is easy to get upset with your bad breaks. Others will sympathize with you if you do. But, do you want sympathy or mental growth? Keep in mind that it will not be bad luck which causes you to develop an incorrect mental attitude. It will only be your attitude toward luck which determines whether the ultimate effect is beneficial or detrimental to the growth of your mental game.

Can you create good luck? It seems that the more skill you develop, the more good luck you have. The more you practice, the luckier you get. Good luck seems to come to those who are best prepared for it. This could be an example of a self-fulfilling prophesy. We seem to get what we expect to get. Expect good luck, prepare for it, anticipate it, and it does seem to appear with some degree of regularity.

However, it is also possible to create your own good luck by deliberately and consciously exposing yourself to comments that could be beneficial to you. There is a never-ending learning process associated with good bowling. Casual comments can often provide useful insights, leading to better understanding of the conditions, your game, or your opponents. It is sometimes very useful to spend time in the bowling center, listening for comments which might be of use to you. Of course, you must be able to properly filter and interpret such comments, but that ability will come with experience.

Superstition is another aspect of luck. The dictionary defines superstition as "a belief or notion, not based upon knowledge, in or of the significance of a particular thing, circumstance, occurrence, proceeding or the like." Superstitions are mental thoughts that we have, some related to good luck and others related to bad luck.

Most of us have some superstitions which we are able to control. Sometimes our superstition is the belief that a certain color is lucky for us, or conversely, that another color is unlucky. We may feel lucky or unlucky (superstitious) about using one particular bowling ball or another.

Although most of our superstitions are unfounded, that is, "not based upon real knowledge", it is important to recognize these feelings and to contend with them. Who is to say that there is no positive feeling gained from accepting a harmless superstition and acting upon it? Perhaps a real psychological lift can be gained by catering to your superstitions. As long as there appears to be no negative impact to the superstition, why not give in to it? After all, what difference does it make what color of clothing you wear? So, if it makes no real difference in affecting the way you deliver the ball, why not wear the color you feel is lucky for you? Or, why not use the ball which you consider lucky?

Real feelings of insecurity and doubt can be created when you do not tend to your superstitions. Such negative feelings can have a negative impact upon your performance on the lanes. So, if you feel lucky doing one thing or another, or wearing one item of clothing, by all means do so. There are many occurrences which cannot be rationally explained, so don't be afraid to recognize your lucky and unlucky superstitions and do something positive about them.

Carrying a good luck charm is also a part of superstition. If you have such a good luck charm, then by all means use it if you think it will give you some mental or physical edge. Most such charms are harmless and do not interfere with your game. Eliminate the guilt feeling about such charms, since it was previously stated that we all have one or more superstitions, even if we don't admit them. If you do feel some guilt, then don't tell anyone about your feelings. There may be positive mental benefits to your superstitions, and you should try to gain such advantages if you can.

In summary, the luck factor is something you have to contend with. It is an integral part of the bowling game, and cannot be eliminated entirely. The presence of the luck factor is not nearly as important as your attitude towards it. A sound mental game is one which has a healthy reaction to both good and bad luck. There will be times when you bowl well and score badly. There will be times when you bowl badly and score well. It is easy to accept good luck for yourself and bad luck for your opponents. However, the proper mental approach to the luck factor is to learn how to graciously accept the good luck of your opponents and the bad luck for yourself.

Stress Seekers enjoy competition.
Stress Avoiders avoid competition.

--- IT IS NOT THE SITUATION THAT DETERMINES WHETHER THE BODY ACTS IN A STRESSFUL MANNER; IT'S YOUR ATTITUDE TOWARD THE SITUATION. ---

This section serves as an introduction to the following two sections. The information in this section is general, providing background information for Sections 8 and 9 which relate more specifically to the mental game of bowling.

Stress is something we all face in everyday life. No one goes through life without facing stressors, stress producing situations. An athlete or competitor faces stress each time he enters competition. Thus, anyone who is serious about his bowling, who plans to compete, should be aware of the sources and symptoms of stress, tension, and anxiety.

These three terms: STRESS, TENSION, and ANXIETY, are often used as though they mean the same thing. There are similarities, but there are also differences in these terms. This section will define these and other terms such as pressure, distress, eustress, and apprehension. With this general background on the subject of stress and its related conditions, the material in Section 8, RELAXATION, and Section 9, CONCENTRATION, should be more meaningful and useful to you.

STRESS is a mentally or emotionally disruptive force or influence. It is a situation or condition which produces actual changes in the chemistry of the body. Stress causes the body to make physiological changes such as an increase in: blood pressure, sugar content of the blood, pulse rate, etc. These changes in the body, and others, are produced in preparation for handling the stressor, the situation which produced the changes.

Our bodies have been conditioned over the centuries to react in an automatic manner to dangers in the environment. Our ancestors, when they were threatened by a wild animal or hostile human, had to immediately and instantaneously prepare to respond. This preparation of the body has been called the "flight or fight syndrome". The previously mentioned physiological changes in the body prepared them for either running from the threat or facing it.

Fortunately, or unfortunately, it is possible for us, by a mere thought process, to create a state of stress which will invoke the flight or fight syndrome. We can create stressful situations by our conscious thought processes. For example, if you begin to think of the economic or other consequences in a competitive situation, you can actually create physiological changes in the body: rushing of blood to the heart, increased heart rate, increased pulse rate, a more rapid flow of adrenalin to all parts of the body, etc. The body prepares for some response.

Stress, therefore, is a change in the body we can create, even when there is no real threat in the environment, similar to the physical dangers which our ancestors might have actually faced. Even though the danger or threat is NOT REAL, the physiological changes in the body ARE REAL, and are exactly the same changes that would take place if we were facing some real threat of physical harm.

The threat is to our psychological body instead of our physical body. A high finish or win in a tournament, plus the possible money to be won, may make a difference in the way we perceive ourselves or in the way others perceive us. There may be a real change in our psychological bodies dependent upon the outcome, perhaps more meaningful to us than a physical change.

It is worth repeating, that situations do not create stress and the accompanying automatic changes in the body. It is YOUR PERCEPTION of the situation which is the determining factor. It is not what happens that determines whether the body will react in a stressful manner, it is your attitude toward what happens. YOU ARE PRIMARILY RESPONSIBLE FOR THE AMOUNT OF PRESSURE AND STRESS YOU FACE.

Some level of increased tension (mental strain, uneasiness) is probably very desirable for most of us. For most people, an increased state of tension will lead to an increased performance level. Giving yourself a "pep talk", "working yourself up", "building your confidence", "arousing your aggressiveness", etc., are all means of increasing the level of personal stress and tension.

At some point, which varies by individual, the tension becomes detrimental to performance. There is a POINT OF DIMINISHING RETURNS. Up to some point, an increase in stress and tension increases our ability to perform. Beyond that point, the increased tension leads to a reduction in performance ability.

An illustration of the concept of the point of diminishing returns can be shown by discussing the tightening of a screw. Up to some point, the more you turn the screw the tighter and more securely it holds. At some point, the additional tightening (tension) strips the screw and it becomes less secure and useless.

Up to some point, stress mobilizes energy and creates the possibility for a higher level of performance. At some point, the added stress tightens (tenses) the muscles and restricts the free flow of movement that is needed for successful athletic performance, (delivering the ball).

This concept of the point of diminishing returns suggests that there are various levels of stress. A low level of stress means that you are not sufficiently aroused to perform at your normal level. You are at a sub-par level of arousal or tension. A "normal" level of stress means that you are sufficiently excited and aroused to perform at your normal skill level. A slightly higher level of stress or tension may give you the temporary ability to perform above your normal level. And, as you go to an even higher level of stress, your normal skills begin to erode. You perform in a manner less than you are capable of performing.

The impact of stress is personal and individualistic. If the stress results in an improvement in performance, it is referred to as EUSTRESS, which literally means "good stress". If the stress causes your abilities to deteriorate, then the stress is referred to as DISTRESS, which means "bad stress". Thus, STRESS is a neutral term with regard to its affect upon performance, since it could result in either above average or below average performance levels.

The same stressful situation can have the opposite impact upon individuals. For some people, stress mobilizes their energies and enables them to perform at a higher level than when the stress is removed. These are called STRESS SEEKERS. For others, stress seems to reduce their energy levels and therefore reduce their ability to perform. These people are called STRESS AVOIDERS. It is important to determine whether you are a person who performs best under pressure or best when pressure is absent. Perhaps a few comments about each type can help you make that determination.

STRESS SEEKERS actively look for competitive situations which will provide them with a healthy amount of "good" stress (really, eustress). They are looking for a sense of danger, something valuable hanging in the balance. The greater the rewards or consequences of the competition (a big prize fund, a great deal of prestige, etc.), the more the opportunity for the stress seeker to gain an invigorating feeling, a sense of exhilaration, a "sports high", so to speak.

It is the competitive challenge which provides the opportunity for a healthy, eustressful feeling. The higher the level of competition, the more the opportunity for feeling good about the competition. Bowlers who are serious about their game, who try to achieve the highest average of which they are capable, who thoroughly enjoy each and every competition, who perform best under some stress, are stress seekers.

STRESS AVOIDERS, on the other hand, are of two types: (1) those who try to avoid competitive situations, or (2) those who perform best when they are NOT under stress. Type one are less competitive by nature, and view competition as a threat. These stress avoiders try to find other ways to find fun and enjoyment, NON-threatening ways. They are not serious bowlers, in the sense that they are not willing to test their skills against other talented bowlers. As long as they are able to roll the ball down the lane, achieve a high game and series on occasion, they are happy. Bowling is not stressful for them, because they will not intentionally seek out stressful situations.

The second type of stress avoider may be a competent bowler, but one who performs best when he is mentally and emotionally calm. He does not need to produce stress and tension to perform well. In fact, he does everything to relax and remain calm during competition. He tries to avoid stress by limiting his thinking to the task at hand, rolling the ball in the best manner he can. This type of stress avoider, and the competent bowler who is a stress seeker, can both be successful.

Stress seekers might use this phrase to get them to perform at their best level on each shot: "There is SOMETHING SPECIAL about this shot". Since this type of person prefers to perform under real or imagined pressure, imagining that each shot is very crucial brings out their best performance.

Stress avoiders who are competent might use this version of the same phrase to calm them down for each frame: "There is NOTHING SPECIAL about this shot". This version of the sentence is designed to develop a "practice mentality" for use in competitive situations. Nothing really does hang in the balance on a practice shot. That is why it is so much easier to perform in practice than in actual competition. If a stress avoider can keep that relaxed practice mentality during competition, he or she should be able to perform at an optimum level.

The concept of an optimum level of anxiety or tension is similar to other factors affecting the body. In moderate amounts, the effect is beneficial. In larger amounts, the effect is detrimental. Both physical and mental aspects of the body can be affected in this manner. Too much stress and tension can have both an impact upon the mind and upon the body, as we will discuss a little later.

Anxiety can be defined as the body's reaction to a situation in which we feel threatened; a pressure situation in which winning or losing are still both possible outcomes. The bodily changes previously mentioned may take place: rapid heart beat, sweating, increase in the pulse rate, a stiffening of the muscles (particularly around the shoulders and neck), etc. Anxiety is a conscious state of worry, a feeling of uneasiness, a sense of apprehension about what is going to happen. When you are anxious, you have an uneasy anticipation of the future in your mind, and your body has undergone some actual chemical changes.

Tension can be thought of as a mental strain; an uneasy suspense. Tension can also be considered an ongoing nervousness, but usually at a much lower level than anxiety. Tension can create anxiety, but may not. It depends upon your mental attitude towards what is causing the tension.

Tension tends to restrict the flow of oxygen to various parts of the body. The blood vessels and smaller capillaries constrict or tighten. Blood flow is reduced to the muscles, which need oxygen to operate properly. This creates a tightening of the muscles, restricting the free movement so necessary for good performance on the lanes. If these tight muscles are in the throat, they (in effect) choke the individual. Thus, a "choke shot" really does result from a choking effect created by tension.

As an illustration of tension and anxiety, suppose you were sitting in the audience and were suddenly asked if you would come to the podium and say a few words. This situation could cause great mental strain on people who are deathly afraid of speaking in front of an audience.

They would become very nervous and anxious, perhaps even fearful. It has caused some people to lose their ability to speak (the vocal cords won't work), or fail to remember their name.

To someone used to speaking to large audiences, who enjoys the opportunity, the tension might still be created, but he or she would approach the podium with a sense of positive anticipation, instead of a sense of dread. And that is the difference in the impact of anxiety on individuals. Those who are tense and anxious, but interpret it in a confident and positive manner, do not suffer any ill effects from the mental strain. Those who interpret the source of the anxiety as threatening, face it with fear and may in fact suffer some ill effects, both physical and mental.

Sometimes the anxiety we feel is at a subconscious level. We are not even aware of the fact that we are anxious. We only become aware of the nervousness after the source of our anxiety has subsided. We reflect back in our thinking and say that we did not even recognize how nervous, anxious, or tense we really were.

Some of the symptoms of subconscious anxiety could include, but not be limited to: an increase in body heat; local sweating or perspiring over the entire body; gnashing or grinding of the teeth; a change in your breathing pattern, including short, shallow breathing or a temporary stoppage of breathing altogether; an unexplained fatigue or tiredness, or muscle stiffness around the neck, shoulders, or upper back. Be alert to the possibility that you may be anxious and not aware of it.

In its more severe forms, stress and anxiety can create a very wide range of detrimental mental and physical conditions. In addition to the ones that were already mentioned, uncontrolled or chronic stress can cause these conditions: an impulsive or irrational behavior which is difficult to explain; migraine headaches, or other types of tension-induced headaches; the inability to sleep properly, or even insomnia; indigestion or heartburn; irritability; apathy, a loss of enjoyment of life, or even depression; increased alcohol or drug use; or an increase in your smoking habit, if you smoke.

In view of the seriousness of some of these changes in the body and the mind, stress is a condition we must be aware of and take definite steps to control. Since eliminating stress from our lives is not a viable option, coping with it is the only answer.

Fortunately, several techniques are available for coping with stress. Before any corrective measures can be taken, you have to recognize that stress is adversely affecting you, identify the sources of the stress, and decide that you are going to correct the situation.

One of the easiest and most effective ways of coping with stress is to learn how to relax. In a later section we will discuss various methods of relaxation, so these techniques will not be repeated at this time. Since relaxation is the opposite of anxiety, any steps you can take to relax yourself will contribute to a lessening of stress and tension.

Sometimes the mere fact that you can talk about and openly discuss your stress with someone whom you trust will help you cope with stress. Rather than keep the stressful situations to yourself, "bottling them up", the stress may be relieved when it is brought out into the open. Often there is not as much reason to become anxious about a situation when we face it openly.

Another way to counteract some of the detrimental effects of stress is to develop and maintain a regular program of exercise, particularly those with aerobic effects (jogging, swimming, tennis, etc.). Exercise gets more oxygen to all parts of the body and has stress-relieving potential for both the mind and body.

The brain is thought to secrete a hormone (called ENDORPHIN) during exercise, which seems to create a sense of well-being without any adverse side effects. Most people who engage in a regular program of exercise feel better, both mentally and physically.

Good nutrition goes a long way toward reducing stress, and the symptoms of stress. If you can get a well-balanced diet of the proper foods, you can help control stress.

Learning to think positively is just another method for coping with stress. The whole idea of a competitive situation is to take anxiety and fear of failure (stressors) which are primarily negative factors, and convert them into positive forces. Dwelling only upon positive thoughts (success and winning), and avoiding all negative thoughts (failure and losing) can considerably reduce the effect of stress.

To conclude, stress, tension, and anxiety, are inherent parts of life in general and competition in particular. Since the focus of this book is the development of a sound mental game for competition, I have limited the discussion of these stress factors to the impact they might have on competitive performance.

Anxiety is a potentially disruptive mental force that can prevent you from achieving your full mental potential. It is a normal part of competitive life, and you have to develop a method of accepting it and keeping it under control.

The reaction to stressors is an evolutionary process, something we have inherited from our ancestors. The major differences between modern anxiety and ancient anxiety, especially in competitive situations, is that flight is not a very realistic option. Coping (fighting) is the only viable answer for anyone who hopes to be a successful competitor.

If you can develop the ability to interpret potentially stressful situations in a non-stressful manner, viewing them as non-threatening, then the normal bodily responses will not be called into play. If the body does not perceive them as important enough to prepare for "fight or flight", then the symptoms of stress will not appear.

There is an optimum level of stress, at which performance is also at an optimum level. Your goal is to reach the level of tension and stress which brings out the best in your performance. Stress is a normal part of competitive life. You simply have to learn how to live with it, to make it useful, to control it instead of letting it control you.

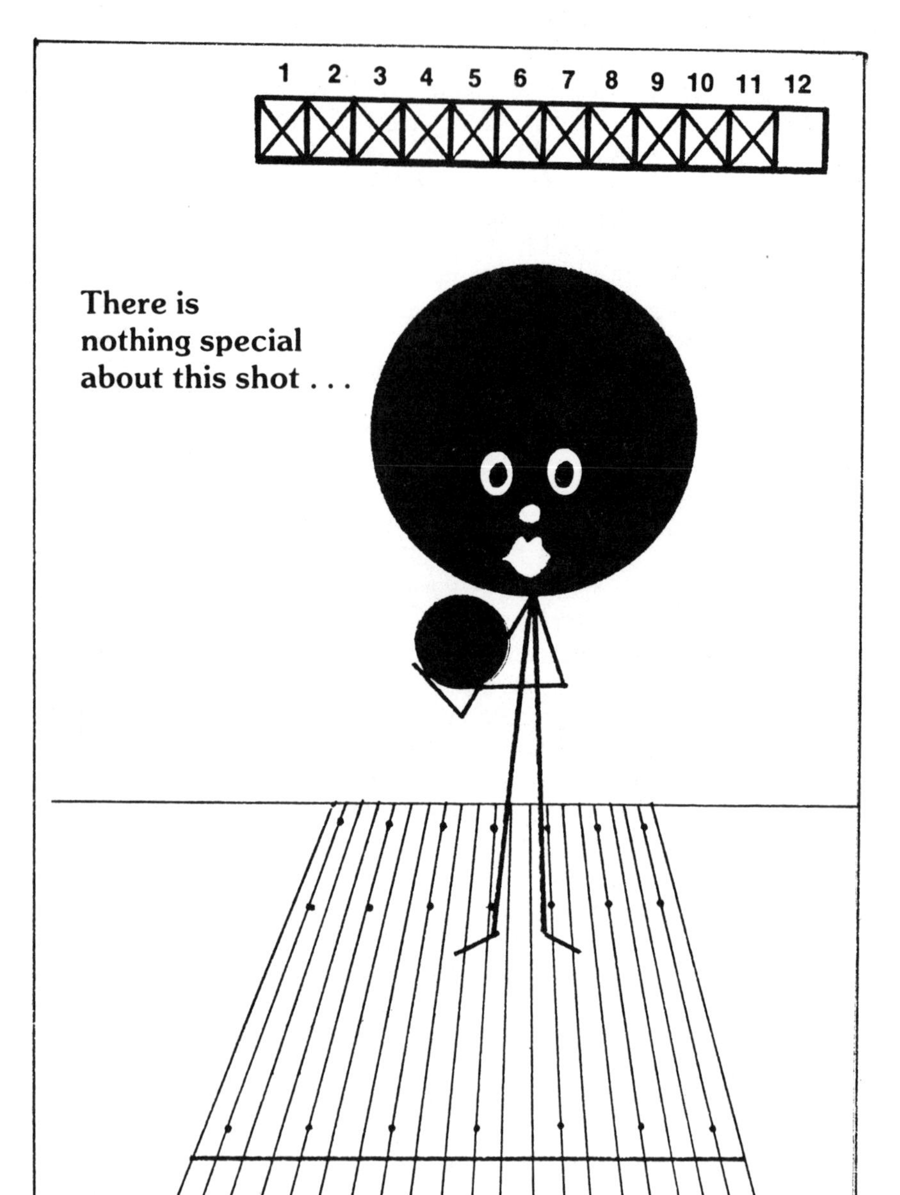

Your best shot in a pressure situation, is your normal approach and delivery.

--- THE BEST SHOT IN A PRESSURE SITUATION IS YOUR NORMAL DELIVERY. ---

What is pressure? How is it created? How do different bowlers react to it? What is the best way to handle pressure? What is your success percentage in pressure situations? Is it 50%, 75% or higher? These questions are of vital importance to every person who is serious about developing mental bowling skills.

Pressure situations are a normal part of all sporting events. There appears to be no way to eliminate such situations, but there are many ways to successfully react to pressure. The purpose of this section is to help you recognize potential pressure situations, and prepare for them well in advance of their occurrence.

A POTENTIAL pressure situation is one in which the consequences of your actions, your performance, are significant to you. A win or loss hangs in the balance. You may win or lose a large sum of money, a league championship, a tournament, etc. Or, on a slightly lower level, when you are in the last frame and need to mark, double, or strike out to win.

In league bowling there is potential for pressure to emerge. A win or loss may depend upon your performance. Your team may be counting on you. Thus, there are win/lose consequences to your actions.

In tournament competition, pressure is potentially at its highest level. Here the penalities for failure or the rewards for success are greatest.

Notice the use of the word POTENTIAL in the preceding paragraphs. The possibility of pressure exists in situations where the consequences of your performance are very significant to you. More specifically, when the losses due to failure are considerable, the potential for pressure is greatest.

ACTUAL pressure is created when you begin to think of the consequences or penalties of your actions, instead of thinking of the actions themselves. It is when winning or losing is on the line, and you think of these possible consequences that you try to override your subconscious mind, and consciously perform what were previously subconscious actions. This is why practice sessions are so different from competitive situations. There are no penalties in practice. Both rewards and penalties are possible in competition.

When you fear failure, your conscious mind does not trust the subconscious mind and tries to help it. You concentrate harder and tension inevitably results. Relaxation becomes more difficult when concentration is intense. And, as you know, bowling is a game requiring relaxed instead of tense muscles.

At this point, some general observations regarding pressure seem clear. Situations do not create tension and pressure: the personal reaction of the participant does. Potentially pressure packed situations will not affect everyone in the same manner. Pressure is created when the thoughts of the person switch from performance to consequences of performance, more specifically, consequences of failure. These principles are important in forming an understanding of the basis of pressure, and to gain insights into how pressure can be handled.

Thus, pressure is both mentally based and self-induced. The person brings pressure upon himself or herself. NO PERSON CAN PUT PRESSURE ON YOU. You will only feel pressure if you let it happen. A person can try to put pressure on you, but ultimately you are the one responsible for your mental state. With proper mental and emotional control, you can decide when you want to feel pressure. If you actually like to feel pressure, if you perform best when you are under pressure, then you can decide when and how much pressure you feel.

The working definition of pressure is: "Pressure is self-induced tension created by thinking about the rewards or punishments of performance instead of the performance itself". Tension and pressure are directly related. When you get tense the muscles become tight, and it is natural to squeeze the ball. There is also a tendency to try to aim the ball, instead of just rolling it naturally and trusting the shot. The result of both squeezing the ball and trying to aim it too much is often a high hit or an ineffective ball if it hits the pocket. The common definition of such a shot is a CHOKE. Or, we say the bowler "choked" on the shot.

Is there any such thing as a CLUTCH SHOT? Yes and no! There will be times when one shot is more important than another. That is, if you strike or convert a spare you win; if not you lose. But, if you are able to TREAT ALL DELIVERIES AS EQUALLY IMPORTANT IN YOUR MIND, then no shot will be considered more important than any other one. This suggests that you should NOT develop a special clutch shot. Your normal delivery is the best one to use at any time. Confidence in your abilities, especially in subconscious execution, will allow you to make no change in a POTENTIAL clutch situation, to deliver the ball in your normal and natural manner. The best way to react to pressure is to DO NOTHING UNUSUAL or different from your normal delivery.

Your ability to ignore potential pressure situations, to treat each frame of each game in exactly the same manner as you treat a practice frame, will determine how much pressure you feel and how you react to it. A statement that might help you achieve this degree of detachment from a potential pressure situation is: THERE IS NOTHING SPECIAL ABOUT THIS SHOT. If you will repeat this statement to yourself while on the approach, and convince yourself that the statement is true, then you may be able to treat each frame equally.

John McEnroe, one of the foremost tennis players in the world, is noted for his ability to handle pressure. He is able to eliminate it entirely, and to quickly get into his ideal mental and physical performance state while on the court.

The role of the conscious mind in any discussion of pressure is of the utmost importance. We have previously stated that PRESSURE IS SELF-INDUCED by consciously thinking about consequences of performance. When pressure situations arise, the conscious mind often takes control of the subconscious mind. This CONSCIOUS MENTAL INTERFERENCE is what causes errors and tension. You concentrate too much, too deliberately, instead of letting the subconscious mind do what it has been trained to do. The conscious mind can NOT do deliberately what the subconscious mind does automatically. (To prove this point, try typing, dancing, or playing a musical instrument, consciously thinking of each key, step, or note, and see how your performance is affected.)

Therefore, if you can DISTRACT YOUR CONSCIOUS MIND during potential pressure situations, and let your normal approach and delivery happen naturally, you should perform well. You have to learn to trust your game, instead of trying to force things to happen.

High-average bowlers react to pressure in one of three ways. Some see pressure as a challenge to be overcome, and they thrive on it. They perform best when pressure is the greatest. They receive a sense of accomplishment for having met a pressure situation head-on and defeated it. Instead of saying "There is nothing special about this shot.", these pressure-seekers say: "There is something very special about this shot."

Others react in an opposite manner. They "choke" or fold under pressure; They are unable to perform in a natural manner when the chips are down. When the potential for success or failure is greatest, they are more apt to consider failure as the outcome. And, failure is often exactly what happens. Such bowlers never achieve all the success their physical game might earn for them, because their reaction to potential pressure stops them.

By far the majority of successful bowlers accept pressure as a normal part of the sport, and learn to live with it. They find ways which allow them to perform well under pressure, or at least as well as they normally perform. They neither benefit from pressure, nor are they intimidated by it. They accept it and learn to cope with it.

If you wish to develop your bowling skills to your maximum potential, you must learn to recognize and handle pressure. Here are a few principles which should make it easier for you to do so.

Develop confidence in your delivery. Pressure will not seem nearly as great if you have confidence in your abilities.

Develop trust in your ability to deliver the ball in a consistent, natural and well-timed manner, and you will feel comfortable and relaxed when tension arises. Confidence can overcome the fear of failure normally associated with pressure situations.

Learn to treat each frame of every game equally. Bowl the frame and not the game. Use the phrase "There is nothing special about this shot" if it works for you. Or, "I'll worry about this shot after it's over" is another saying that might help. Concentrate on your delivery and perfect execution of the shot in each frame, trying to forget previous or future frames. If you make your best shot in every frame, there is nothing more you can do, and nothing you need be concerned about.

Consider tension and pressure as mental faults which you are going to eliminate from your game. (Faults will be discussed in Sections 14 and 15.) Such faults can be corrected by locating and eliminating the sources of the problems. Since pressure and tension are self-induced (created by the bowler), the solution lies within the person.

Learn to bowl in a relaxed manner at all times. Tension is an enemy of good bowling. Taking a deep breath in potential pressure situations will help you relax. It is difficult to remain tense when you are breathing deeply.

Focus attention on your target on the lane each time you bowl. AIMING HELPS TO DISTRACT THE CONSCIOUS MIND. Concentrate on that target, and your conscious mind will not interfere with the normal delivery of the ball. One professional bowler sings to himself to distract his mind, and to relax himself during pressure situations. Others prefer to enter a semi-trance state while bowling (using elements of self-hypnosis), or concentrating deeply upon their game or upon something completely different. There is no single best way to distract the conscious mind so the subconscious mind can perform naturally, but concentrating on your target is a good method.

Simulate or pretend that you are under pressure while you are practicing. Use your wonderful imagination. Pretending may not be as beneficial as the real thing, but it can help prepare you for real pressure when it occurs. Remember: the mind is not able to distinguish between a real experience and one that is imagined or visualized with a great deal of clarity. Imagine yourself needing three strikes to win an important match or game. Pretend you need to convert a spare for a tie. Pretend your opponent has made a double and you need two strikes to keep up with him or her. These simulated or imaginary situations, if vividly imagined, can get your mind thinking as it might during times when these situations actually occur, as they will.

Put yourself into as many competitive situations as possible. Pressure situations are abnormal situations that occur frequently in competition. The more of them you encounter, the more normal they become. The more normal they become, the more likely you are to bowl in your natural manner in these situations.

Use your same relaxed delivery on every shot, forgetting about the potential consequences. DON'T DEVELOP A SPECIAL CHOKE SHOT. No matter how many strikes you have strung together, the best shot on your next frame is your normal relaxed shot.

And finally, a mental technique for handling pressure is to accentuate the positive and eliminate the negative. When faced with a pressure situation, if you must think of the consequences of your actions, think positively. Think of success and the rewards of winning. But, preferably, think only of perfect execution.

In conclusion, pressure situations are a normal part of the mental game of bowling or any other sport, especially at the higher competitive levels. The ability to compete under pressure is the hallmark of the truly outstanding bowler, and is a test of personal self-control and mental growth.

Pressure and tension are self-induced; they are consciously created in the mind of the person feeling the pressure. Therefore, they can be controlled by that person, if that person has learned to control his or her emotions.

If you are to achieve the status of a high-average bowler, one who is successful in a wide variety of competitive situations, you will have to accept, recognize, face and conquer pressure. And you can, if you will put into practice all of the principles for handling pressure which are outlined above.

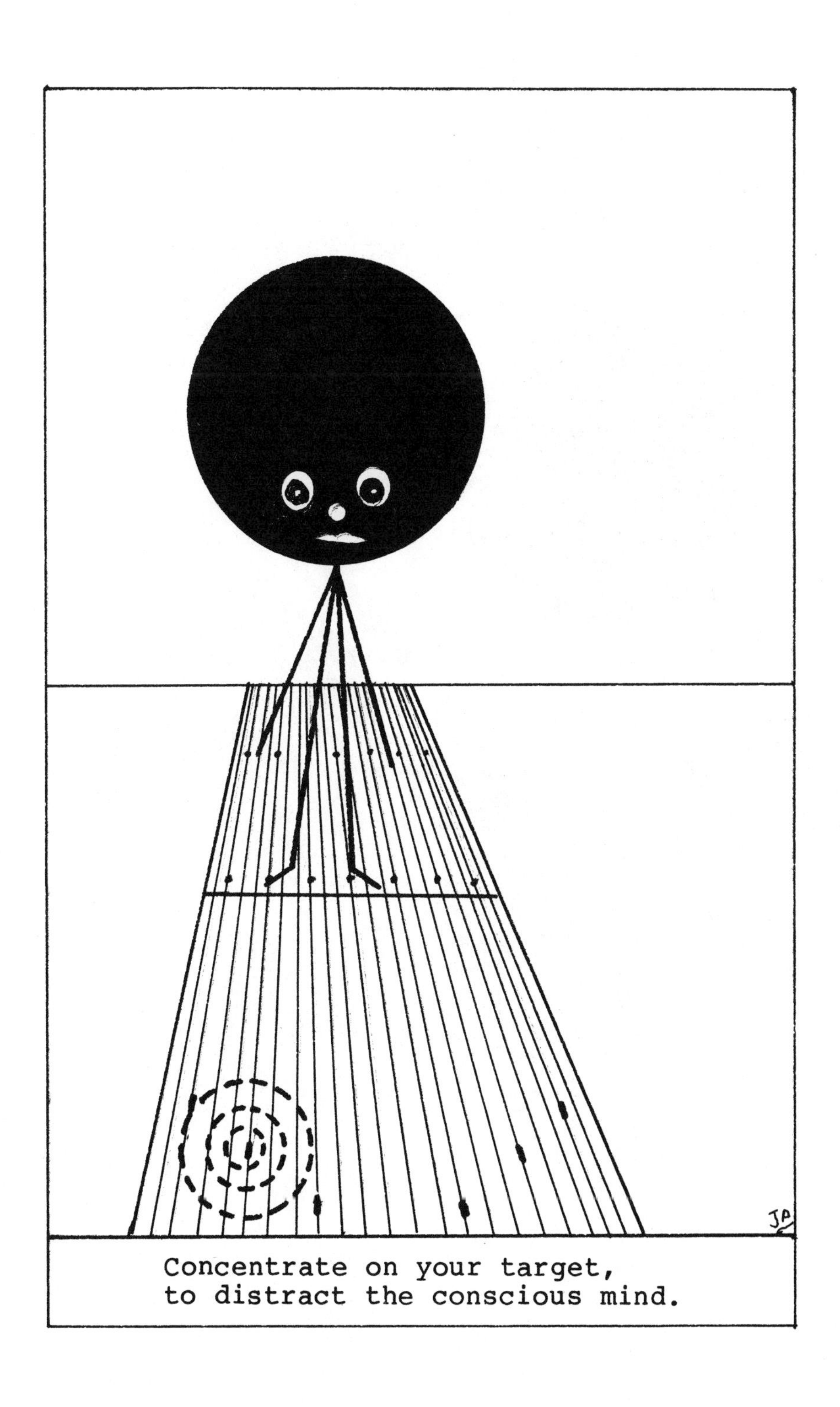

Concentrate on your target,
to distract the conscious mind.

Self-hypnosis is a useful technique for learning how to relax.

--- THE PLAYER OF THE INNER GAME COMES TO VALUE THE ART OF RELAXED CONCENTRATION, ABOVE ALL OTHER SKILLS --- Timothy Gallwey

Relaxation and concentration are two essential elements in a well-developed mental game. Relaxation will be discussed in this section, and concentration will be the topic for the next section. The above quote should explain the reasoning behind the decision to place these two topics together. The kind of concentration that is best for effective bowling is the kind that is relaxed instead of tense.

As mentioned in Section 5, LET IT HAPPEN NATURALLY, tension is the enemy of good bowling; relaxation is the ally. The purpose of this section is to review some of the benefits of achieving a relaxed state.

It is not possible to fully explain all the relaxation techniques which exist. Books have been written about each one. Instead, I would like to highlight the main features of two or three, and suggest sources of the best information to explore the whole subject of relaxation.

This section will consist of three topics: (1) The Purpose of Relaxation Exercises, (2) Biofeedback techniques, and (3) Transcendental Meditation (called TM for short). In the concluding paragraphs I will briefly mention self-hypnosis, another method for achieving a relaxed state.

THE PURPOSE OF RELAXATION TECHNIQUES: The purpose of all autogenic (good health) training techniques such as biofeedback, transcendental meditation (TM), and other relaxation methods is SELF-MASTERY. The objective is to enable you to master your mental or emotional state of mind, which indirectly gives you control over your body.

In a relaxed state you can rejuvenate the body and synchronize the mental and physical parts of the body; you can rest both mentally and physically. You put yourself in the position of being able to take full advantage of whatever skills you possess. Relaxation enhances the natural process of self-development. It accelerates this development. It allows each individual to benefit, on a personal basis, from the use of the technique. Therefore, the full development of the individual is really the ultimate objective of most relaxation techniques, especially TM.

The state of relaxation required for maximum performance on the lanes cannot co-exist with a state of anxiety, fear or tension. Anxiety and relaxation are feelings that are mutually exclusive; both cannot exist at the same time. To the extent that outside pressures are allowed to affect the body and reduce the feeling of relaxation, the pleasure of competition and chances of winning are both diminished.

Being relaxed during competition does not mean you are unconcerned about winning, that you are taking for granted that you will perform well and win. A strong desire to win and a relaxed attitude can co-exist. A relaxed attitude gives the desire to win a better chance of happening. It is a matter of putting your focus of attention in the right place. If you concentrate, in a relaxed manner, on executing each shot in each frame, you should perform as well as you can. If you perform as well as you can, quite obviously, there is nothing more you can do to assure a successful tournament.

And if you can maintain this relaxed frame of mind and body during competition, you will be satisfied with your performances more often than not.

One of the concepts mentioned in MENTAL JUDO (listed in the Bibliography) is that of "energy conservation". The purpose of energy conservation is to save your energy so you can be more relaxed and flexible. This allows you to maintain both physical and mental sharpness when you have to bowl many games. You will be less likely to become tense, pressure will have less effect upon you, and you should be able to keep an attitude of relaxed concentration. The idea, of course, is to conserve your energy by using as little of it as possible. (Those of you who have difficulty with stamina might find this book useful.)

Physical changes occur in the body when you are NOT relaxed. These can be corrected by using any of the relaxation techniques. It is possible to achieve, through relaxation, a decreased metabolic state of 15% to 20% of your normal level (a deep state of rest). Such a relaxed state is the opposite of the flight or fight state, when adrenalin is flowing and the body is poised for action.

High lactic blood levels can trigger anxieties. If you are able, by conscious relaxation techniques, to reduce lactic levels, you can reduce anxiety. You can see that relaxation techniques are designed to deliberately change the physical state of the body, as well as change the mental state.

The discussions which follow will of necessity be somewhat technical. Certain terms must be used to adequately describe the techniques. However, it is possible to learn these relaxation methods with no additional background or preparation. Most of the books I recommend for additional reading are written in a straight-forward manner.

BIOFEEDBACK: The state of the mind and the state of the body are very closely interconnected. A change in one creates a change in the other. Biofeedback is one process which gives you the ability to deliberately create changes in your body, or prevent such changes, by conscious thought processes.

One example of a biofeedback technique in action (previously mentioned) is to tell yourself prior to every shot that there is either NOTHING special about this shot, or SOMETHING SPECIAL about it. The objective of the statement is to either get your body relaxed or aroused, depending upon whether you are a stress-avoider or stress-seeker, as discussed in Section 7. This statement is a deliberate, conscious act designed to cause the body to reduce or create tension for the shot. For most people, on a long string of strikes, it is best to keep the body relaxed so you can deliver the ball in your normal manner.

Biofeedback is the ability to become sensitive to the psychological (mental) and physiological (chemical) states of the body. You become aware of your pulse rate and respiration, your thought processes, blood pressure, etc. Once you can tune-in to these processes, you can develop the ability to alter them, to control what were previously considered non-controllable reactions of the body. (Mike Lastowski, the 1983 ABC Masters Champion, checked his pulse regularly during each match of the competition.)

Every time there is a change in the state of the mind, there is a change in the state of the body. The reverse is also true; a change in the body produces a change in the state of the mind. For example, if you become tense in any competitive situation, your heart rate, breathing rate, and your perspiration rate, would probably all be affected.

Obviously, any change in bodily processes, such as increased adrenalin flow, quickened pulse, more rapid heart beat, can be sensed. Through biofeedback techniques you can heighten your sensitivity to these processes. With increased awareness you then learn methods for controlling them.

People who are competent in biofeedback techniques have been able to raise or lower their blood pressure at will, by deliberately and consciously telling the body to do so! This is similar in concept to you telling your body to raise your right hand. You know you can do this. But, to deliberately change blood pressure was thought to be a process over which we had no conscious control.

A closed biofeedback loop is created when you learn how to interpret body signals and to send a message to change these signals. By using positive thinking, concentration, self-hypnosis, and other relaxation methods, you can control your pulse rate, your rate of breathing, and other reactions the body might have to stress and pressure.

Biofeedback is sometimes referred to as "brain learning". This is a method by which you can consciously affect brain wave patterns, in addition to blood pressure, respiratory rate, pulse rate, etc. Most of these body reactions are normally controlled by the autonomic nervous system, not by conscious thought processes. Biofeedback gives you the ability to consciously control these automatic or subconscious processes.

This means that if you are getting tense and becoming distressed, if your pulse rate and heart rate are rising, you are able to stop these processes by conscious thought. You can alter these so-called automatic body processes. If you enter a situation that you perceive as threatening, the adrenalin will automatically surge throughout the body, preparing you for a fight or flight response. It is possible, with biofeedback, to alter that process.

People trained in biofeedback techniques have a heightened awareness of their bodies and the functions of their bodies. They use their sensitivity to bring about relaxation, which permits a healthy adjustment to the environment.

Biofeedback techniques usually require some clinical equipment, setting a limit on the use of the technique outside of the laboratory. However, the concept does not have to work completely to bring about some favorable change. Some relaxation, properly timed, is much better than none.

The concept of conscious control over our body's reaction to potentially stressful situations means that you can decide, to some extend, how you will respond to changes in the environment. It means that you are not at the mercy of automatic body changes; you can control them. For example, you can control the extent to which pressure situations affect you. You can, in fact, decide if you will feel any pressure in potential pressure situations. You have a choice to become tense or relaxed. A knowledge of biofeedback methods can free you from the unfounded thought that you are at the mercy of automatic body reactions. You can learn how to control your body and its reactions.

TRANSCENDENTAL MEDITATION: The use of transcendental meditation (referred to only as TM) is another way to induce relaxation. TM was introduced in the United States at the beginning of the decade of the 1960's, by Maharishi Mehesh Yogi. Devotees of TM consider this the only or best method for achieving mental growth and development.

From a single individual, the ideas spread rapidly. Now there is an organization called the AAPPTMP, American Association of Physicians Practicing the Transcendental Meditation Program, which claims over 6,000 PHYSICIANS as members. Some of the member physicians claim that TM has an impact on the aging process, causing it to slow down.

This discussion of TM will be brief, restricted to the use of TM in attaining relaxation, and summarize its main features. For those of you who wish to explore the subject in more depth, there are books on the subject listed in the Bibliography.

The ultimate goal of TM is the full development of human potential. It is a relaxation and meditation technique, that is characterized by three factors separating TM from other relaxation techniques: (1) A DEEP REST, much different from a deep sleep and attained more quickly, (2) MENTAL ALERTNESS, a wakeful hypo-metabolic state, and (3) an ORDERLINESS OF MENTAL AND PHYSICAL ACTIVITIES.

TM produces a deep sleep effect, reducing the metabolism of the body to perhaps 20% of normal. It usually takes from 6 to 7 hours to reach this level of rest when you go to sleep. With TM, you should be able to reach the deep rest state of relaxation very quickly, from a few minutes to less than one hour. This ability to achieve a deep rest explains why people using TM feel rested after a FEW MINUTES.

You are more mentally alert in TM than when you are sleeping. While sleeping, you are more unconscious and not very alert. In TM, you are considered to be in a restful, alert state, in a wakeful, hypo-metabolic state. The body functions have been slowed down, like a bear or other animal that is in hybernation.

Brain wave patterns are affected by TM. Alpha, beta, delta, and theta brain wave patterns are more in harmony in a TM state. When these brain waves have been synchronized, a more restful state of mind exists. In effect, TM is able to quiet the brain, to de-excite it; a desirable effect in potential pressure situations. Increased mental and physical orderliness is only one of the benefits ascribed to the use of TM.

Transcendental meditation uses a MANTRA: "A sound, the effects of which are known". The sound of the mantra, which is repeated during the TM session, is used to remove all thoughts from the mind in order to produce a relaxed state.

You cannot produce this relaxed state simply by telling yourself to relax. You cannot tell the mind to remove all thoughts. The use of the mantra, a WORD or SYLLABLE you repeat over and over again, is designed to distract the mind from thinking so that relaxation will occur naturally.

According to advocates of TM, the mantra is a sound or word given to the TM student by his or her teacher. Some TM advocates feel that the mantra must be known only to the student and the teacher (a secret between them), while others feel that the mantra can be developed by the student for himself. Herbert Benson, author of THE RELAXATION RESPONSE, says that it is not necessary to have an instructor give the student the mantra. You can, according to Benson, create your own mantra and use it just as effectively as if one were assigned to you.

The function instead of the source of the mantra should be the critical factor. If the mantra does what it is supposed to do, then it should not matter where it originated.

The mantra is not supposed to produce any thoughts, such as would occur if you repeated Alcatraz, Statue of Liberty, New York, or other words or phrases. A mantra is supposed to block out all thoughts, so relaxation can occur. A mantra is supposed to establish a harmonious sound which echoes or reverberates throughout the body. The mantra sets up a harmonic resonance within the body, creating "good vibes", good vibrations throughout the body.

Sound affects the body in various ways. A mother can hear her infant cry even when the mother is asleep. Most people can hear the sound of their name in a noisy room, even if they are engaged in a conversation and not listening to the conversation in which their name is spoken.

The sound of a siren, screeching of brakes, and applause are only three examples of sound that will produce some effect on the body. Music might put some people to sleep. Thus, the use of a mantra to generate the effects of sound on the body is scientifically based.

You are NOT supposed to be thinking while repeating your mantra. Thoughts will try to enter your mind. Try only to think of the mantra and nothing else. Let whatever happens in your mind simply happen. This is another example of the concept of LETTING IT HAPPEN NATURALLY. You can't force a state of relaxation to occur; you can only create the situation in which it can happen, and get out of the way and let it happen naturally.

TM and other meditation techniques should not be classified or equated with religious activities. They should not be viewed in a religious context, since that may discourage people from trying them. (The initial start with Maharishi Mehesh Yogi probably accounts for this religious connection.)

General relaxation techniques can contribute to your mental growth and development. They have much to offer any competitor, especially one who wants to master the mental game. William Glasser, author of POSITIVE ADDICTION, considers meditation one of the best means of achieving relaxation, and one of the best things to which you can become addicted.

There is obviously much more to transcendental meditation that can be covered in this brief section. For those of you who wish to pursue the subject in depth, please read TM AND BUSINESS, listed in the Bibliography.

In concluding this section on relaxation techniques, I would like to briefly touch upon self-hypnosis. This relaxation method, like transcendental meditation, offers a method for controlling body functions which were previously thought to be beyond conscious control, including: heart rate, pulse rate, reaction to pain, respiration rate, etc.

C. Eugene Walker, author of the book LEARN TO RELAX, defines self-hypnosis as "A heightened state of consciousness, accompanied by an increased ability to act on ideas and suggestions". He relates hypnosis to a continuum (a line), on which the two extremes are Distraction and Concentration. Under self-hypnosis, you are able to concentrate more effectively; your attention can be focused and channeled more precisely.

Self-hypnosis offers three benefits to serious bowlers: FIRST, is an ability to train the subconscious mind. As noted in Section 1 and Section 2, the development of subconscious competence is the means of reaching your full potential. SECOND, you can use self-hypnosis to learn how to relax. It is an effective technique, and relatively easy to learn. High-level performance is achieved most often when muscles are relaxed. THIRD, using self-hypnosis, you can divert the conscious mind when it is time to deliver the ball. The conscious mind is then unable to interfere with the normal delivery, which is particularly important in potential pressure situations.

Self-hypnosis is a method of creating a deep sense of concentration. It is also possible to develop an ability to focus your concentration solely upon the single delivery you are making, forgetting all previous frames and with no thought of future frames. (BOWL THE FRAME AND NOT THE GAME, is the essence of good bowling.)

Self-hypnosis can create an "altered state of consciousness", a method of re-distributing and concentrating your energies. It is easier to concentrate under self-hypnosis; there is less tendency to become distracted with events happening in the environment.

A TRANCE-LIKE state is created with self-hypnosis. Glenn Allison, who rolled the disputed perfect 900 series, mentioned that after it was over he felt like he had been in a trance. Paul Moser, who shot 300-279-300 = 879, mentioned a trance-like state in Chuck Pezzano's column in BOWLING magazine (January, 1983). Moser stated: "When you get grooved-in you can and probably should fall into what I call TRANCE BOWLING." (Self-hypnosis, however, does NOT mean putting yourself in a trance, and bowling that way.)

Some athletes who have lost their confidence have turned to hypnosis (not self-hypnosis) to recapture it. Sometimes the reason for the lack of confidence is based in the subconscious, and hypnosis is a good way to locate and remove these types of problems. What psychologists look for are mental blocks or barriers which the athletes have developed. Once found, the hypnotist (psychologist) can prescribe ways of removing these impediments from the mind.

Some psychologists think that most athletes who have prolonged slumps are suffering from psychological problems of a subconscious nature. Through hypnosis, they can be found and corrected.

Jack Heise has written a very interesting and useful book that is particularly good for bowlers, called HOW YOU CAN BOWL BETTER USING SELF-HYPNOSIS. If you want to explore self-hypnosis in more detail, this book should answer all your questions. Also, you can often find tapes on the process of self-hypnosis in your local library which are free and usually very good.

If you would like more information on a specific way to relax, two books you might want to read are: DON'T CHOKE, and THE RELAXATION RESPONSE. These books are listed in the Bibliography, and are probably available at your local library.

Finally, keep in mind that you are trying to find a relaxation technique that will work for you, because bowling is (as I have stated so often) a game of relaxed muscles. It does not matter what technique you use, nor does the technique have to be perfect to be beneficial. Some relaxation is better than none. As long as you can teach yourself to relax the mind and body, you will be getting the desired result, and will be greatly improving your mental game.

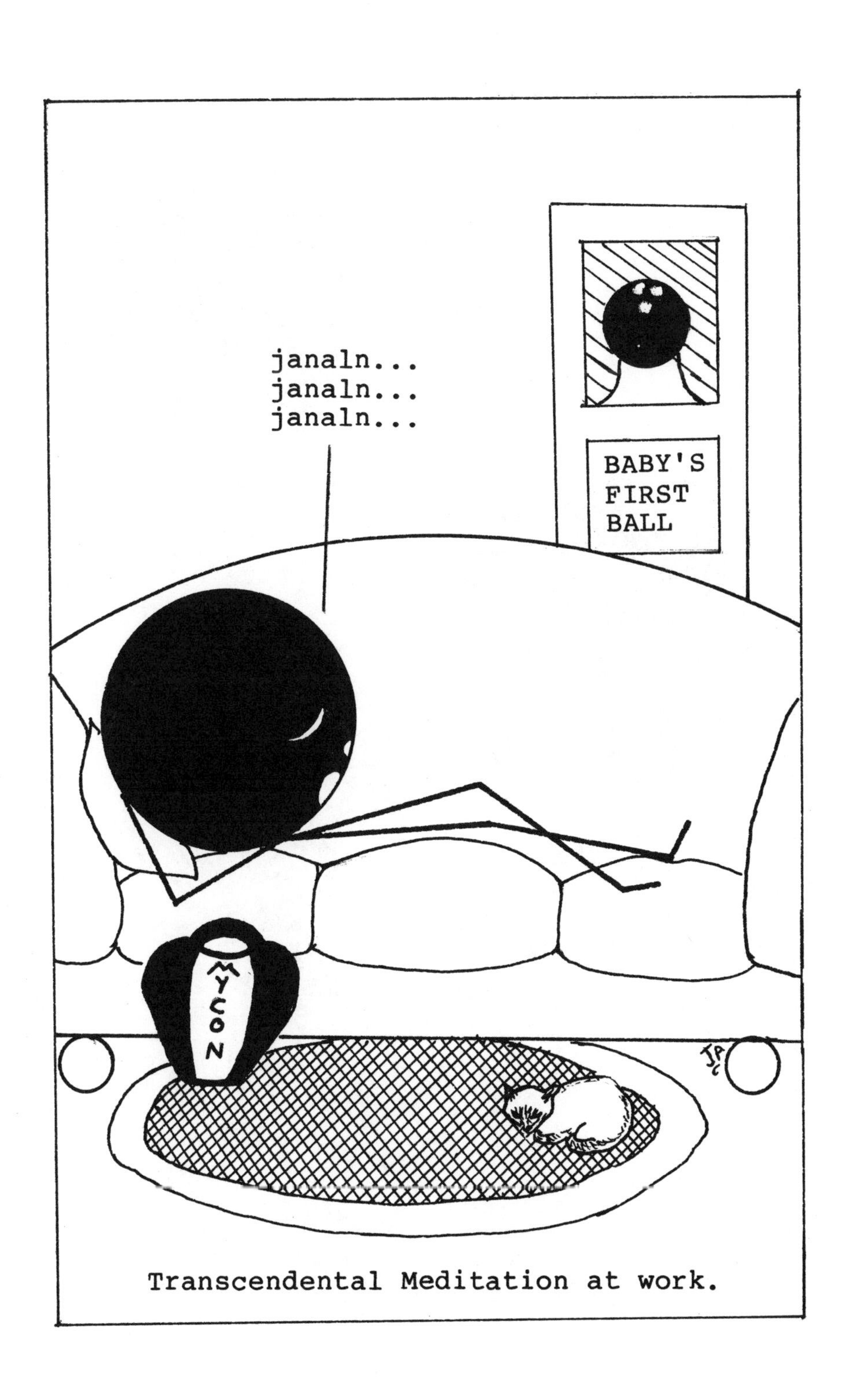

Transcendental Meditation at work.

Distract the conscious mind, and let the subconscious mind deliver the ball.

--- CONCENTRATE TO DISTRACT THE CONSCIOUS MIND, AND LET THE SUBCONSCIOUS MIND DELIVER THE BALL. ---

Concentration is the ability to focus attention, wants, desires, and thought processes, on a single item. Concentration is an essential talent for achieving success in any athletic endeavor. For bowling, concentration means the ability to focus all your attention on the feeling of lift as the ball comes off the fingers. It also means concentrating on any other aspect of the approach or delivery, height of the ball in the backswing, location of the ball at all times during the approach, etc. And, it also means the ability to keep your eyes firmly fixed upon your target on the lanes from the time the ball is placed in motion (the pushaway) until the ball has passed over or by the target.

Concentration is the ability to isolate all external distractions from what you are doing, and block them from your conscious mind. You are able to place yourself in a vacuum, with all your thoughts channeled into what you are doing; in this case, delivering a ball down the lane. If you are concentrating well, you can focus all your attentions on a single item.

A golfer only hits the ball, using either a wood, an iron, or a putter. This is all he or she does. Once the ball leaves the club head, the golfer has no control over its flight path or where it eventually stops rolling. Thus, the golfer like the bowler must focus all his energies and concentration on the only thing he or she does: hit (deliver) the ball.

The mental game comes into play in deciding what club to use, whether to try for a slice, fade or straight shot, where the ball should land and stop, how hard to hit the ball, etc. Notice that the mental game comes into play before the ball is hit. After that, it is up to the fates to decide where the ball goes.

A golfer concentrates by keeping his eyes on the ball. A bowler concentrates by keeping his eyes on the target. Both these efforts are identical in purpose: DISTRACT THE CONSCIOUS MIND SO THE SUBCONSCIOUS MIND CAN EXECUTE THE SHOT. The more effectively you can get the conscious mind out of the way, the more likely you are to hit your normal shot. Of course, full concentration (full distraction of the conscious mind) is particularly necessary when the shot is in a crucial situation.

The book SELF-PSYCHING mentions a useful concept called "thought stopping". When your mind is flooded with ideas, some of which are conflicting and others negative, it is valuable to be able to control the flow of these ideas into your mind. Self-defeating or negative thoughts undermine confidence. Preventing them from entering the mind is one way to maintain self-confidence.

Thoughts flooding the mind are at the conscious level. As such, they may be easier to control. When you are ready to tee off in golf, serve in tennis, or deliver the ball in bowling, you want to stop all conscious thoughts from entering the mind. Ideally, you want no thoughts in your mind at all, which was discussed as part of the transcendental meditation method of relaxation in Section 9. You want to get all conscious thoughts out of your mind and perform subconsciously.

Concentration on a single item, the ball in golf or tennis, the target in bowling, is an effective way to block the flow of thoughts into the mind. Relaxation techniques such as transcendental meditation and self-hypnosis have as their objective, control over the flow of thoughts to the mind.

You can practice thought-stopping while you are jogging, or doing any other aerobic exercise. Often, when I am jogging, I will have to use the technique to distract my conscious mind, to let me get the maximum mileage from my jogging program. My mind will start to think about all the reasons why I should stop jogging: my legs ache; my feet are tired; I have already gone three miles; my back is sore; etc. By diverting my thoughts to other areas, by working on some mental problems while I am jogging, I can forget about these real or imagined ailments and continue to jog for greater distances.

The eye is fascinated by movement. If something moves, it captures your attention automatically, unless you have learned to ignore such distractions. This explains a source of difficulty in bowling. The target on the lanes is stationary, but the ball is moving over it. It takes practice to keep your eyes on the target when the ball is moving and other things are moving in the center.

One way to achieve this ability to concentrate on your stationary target is to go to the lanes and select one of the five target-finders embedded in the lane. Try to look at that target, that arrow, for a full minute without noticing anything else in the center. Don't take your eyes off it; don't think about anything else; ignore everything that is happening around you.

Practice the habit of concentrating on a single spot on the lanes while others are bowling. In your practice sessions, try keeping your eyes on the target until the ball is in the pit. Select a dark or light board, or any distinct spot on the lane. The objective is to be able to focus all your attention on a single spot on the lanes when there are many distractions around you. You could even practice this exercise in concentration in your home, selecting any object to stare at for a minute or more, although it is better to practice in the center where there are more distractions.

If you have difficulty concentrating on such a small target, take the process in gradual stages. Select an area between two arrows, a five board spread. Once it is easy to focus on that broad area, narrow it down to two boards. Then to a single board, and then to a crack between two boards. Pick a spot about 15 feet down the lanes and practice looking at it. Pick another one about 40 feet down the lanes. Do not strain to concentrate on these spots. Try to REMAIN RELAXED WHILE YOU ARE CONCENTRATING.

You are practicing four essential parts of the delivery when you are learning how to focus your attentions on a spot on the lanes: (1) you should be able to hit your target more often if you are able to concentrate on it; (2) you should be able to block negative thoughts from entering your mind while you are bowling; (3) you should be able to overcome the natural tendency of the eyes to follow motion; and (4) you are learning how to get the conscious mind out of the way while your subconscious mind is delivering the ball.

Your competitors may be a source of distraction, interfering with your ability to concentrate. Watching your competitors may create unnecessary pressure for you. If they are doing well, you may begin to try too hard. If they are doing poorly, you may tend to relax and not give your best effort. In either case, you have not helped your game at all.

Instead of keeping an eye on what others are doing, focus all your attention on your own game. You CANNOT control what others are doing, so don't let it concern you. Also, if you perform as well as you can, you have done all you can to win.

Some people, however, bowl best when they know what they have to do to win. If you are that type of person, then by all means use this method to bring out the best in your performances. If, however, watching your competition distracts from your own concentration, then remove this source of distraction.

Sometimes you will be bowling an opponent who is not scoring well. You may begin to lose your concentration, to bowl less than your normal average. To avoid this mental lapse, first be alert to the possibility and redouble your concentration on your delivery. You might even set a target score for yourself, a personal goal to strive for. Concentrate on perfect execution on each delivery.

Setting your own goal when the one you are facing (a win) appears to be relatively certain, keeps gentle pressure on yourself and prevents a mental lapse. Keep your concentration relaxed and intact on every shot of every frame, and you will reach your full scoring potential.

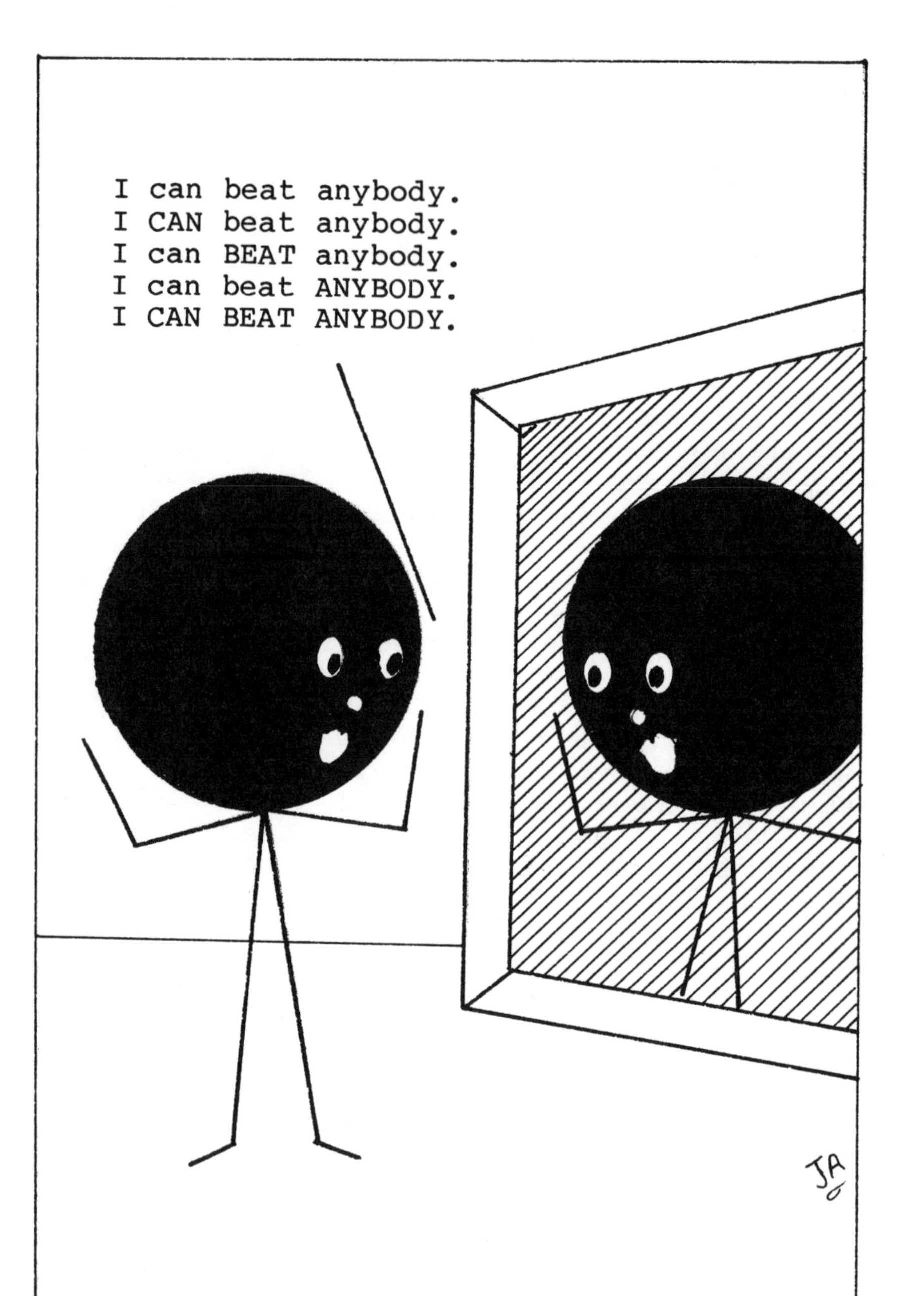

Sometimes a "pep talk" with yourself is all that is needed to psych yourself up.

--- PSYCHING YOURSELF UP MEANS MENTALLY PREPARING TO PERFORM AT YOUR BEST LEVEL ---

Perhaps one of the most widely accepted principles of the mental game as it applies to any sport is that performance is best when the individual's motivation is at an optimum level. In an individualistic sport such as bowling, where performance is based upon your own skills, it is necessary to arouse yourself, to raise your level of aggression and motivation to the peak level for you. It is difficult for anyone else to do this for you; you must do it for yourself.

It is important to assess your emotional or mental state prior to each competitive situation. You need to know what your optimum level of stress or tension is, and whether you are at that "peak". If you have not reached the optimum level for your best performance, if you are not sufficiently psyched-up, then you need to take steps to reach a higher stress level. If you are too psyched-up, then you need to do something to calm yourself down.

Implied in the concept of psyching yourself up is an effort to create a heightened awareness of the situation, your mental and physical state, and perhaps some thought about your opponent. Psyching yourself up means mentally preparing yourself to perform at your best level.

Bowling against a top player can have two possible psychological effects. One is to cause you to be intimidated and to bowl poorly. The other mental reaction is to cause you to rise to the occasion, to bowl your best. Earl Anthony seems to bring out this response in his competitors. He loses many matches because his opponents get psyched-up against him and bowl well. But, Anthony scores so well even when he may be losing the match, that he does not lose many pins even in losing. His consistent high average keeps him in the competition, despite a normally poor won-loss record in match play.

I mentioned an optimum level for performance. When the need arises, you should be able to either increase the adrenalin flow to meet the occasion, or to reduce the flow to calm yourself. To achieve this, you might use biofeedback techniques or other mental stimulation or relaxation techniques discussed in Section 9.

The goal is mental control, to try to stabilize the mental game so it is always within a given range: not high enough to create negative anxiety, nor low enough to reduce effectiveness.

The chart on page 105 illustrates the objective of psyching yourself up or down. Emotions will fluctuate before, during and after competition. Your goal, for complete mental control, is to prevent your emotions from either going too high (too keyed-up) or falling too low (not keyed-up enough).

Some bowlers prefer to psych themselves up for competition; they thrive on the flow of adrenalin. Others perform best when they are calm, with little or no tension or anxiety. You must find your optimum level for performance, and develop the mental game that will let you take your emotions to that level.

The center line represents the normal equilibrium, or balance, of emotions around

OPTIMUM RANGES FOR MENTAL AND EMOTIONAL CONTROL

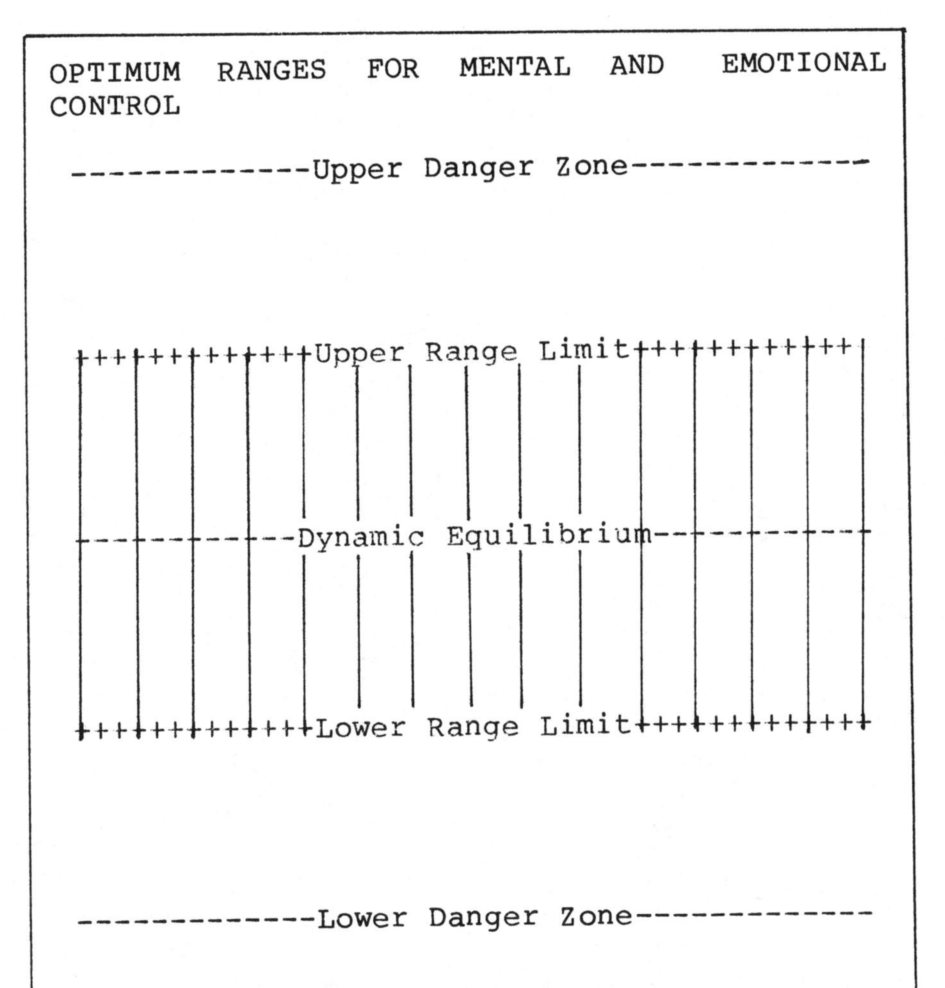

Your emotions will fluctuate before, during and after competition. There are ways to control this fluctuation, to keep your emotions within your Optimum Zone.

Your objective, in psyching yourself either up or down, is to keep your emotions within this Optimum Zone while you are making your delivery, and prevent them from rising too high or falling too low.

which your emotions should revolve. At times you may want to arouse yourself to a higher emotional level. At other times you want to de-arouse yourself, calm yourself.

How accurately can the upper and lower limits of the optimum range be defined? Not very precisely. The concept is important, not the degree of precision anyone might try to use to define the limits.

Each person is an individual, and should know when his or her mental state is ideal for effective performance. Learning to recognize when you are outside the optimum range, and knowing how to get your emotions back into that range, are two facets of the emotional control aspect of the mental game. This is another reason why the mental game is so difficult to master, if it is possible to master it at all.

With this background in mind, and with the graphic concept of an optimum range for emotions, we can now be a little more specific about psyching yourself up or down.

PSYCHING YOURSELF UP for competition involves both psychological (mental) and physiological (body) adjustments. Changes of a psychological nature involve your mental outlook, such as confidence level, temperament, attitude, aggression level, etc. Physiological changes are such bodily changes as increased heart rate, more rapid breathing, increased adrenalin flow, etc.

Since bowling is a game that is executed best when muscles are relaxed, a normal physiological balance is generally conceded to be the best condition for effective performance. That is, the heart rate, breathing, pulse, etc. should be as close to normal as possible. Remember, your normal approach and delivery is the best shot you can make at any time, under any competitive situation.

The body produces adrenalin in preparation for fight or flight situations. If you are sufficiently psyched-up, the flow of adrenalin will be sufficient to insure a normal level of COMPETITIVE AGGRESSION. If you are not sufficiently aroused, you should take positive steps to get the adrenalin flowing.

A "pep talk" with yourself can be a useful way to arouse yourself in preparation for competition. You might take some time alone and think positive thoughts. Use your imagination to think of the rewards of success, or just think about your game and visualize a series of successful deliveries. (Section 16 discusses several visualization techniques.)

If you do not like to inflict a loss on anyone, you may have to psych yourself up by focusing your attention on the pins. Pretend you want to knock them all down, all the time, which is exactly what you want to do anyhow.

On the other hand, if you like to defeat your opponents, focus your attention on them. Imagine them being out to beat you and you are going to beat them to the punch. Work up an aggressive feeling toward them.

Some bowlers like to psych themselves up by drilling a new ball for each new competition. It is like a fresh start each time. But, others like the security and predictability of a ball they have used for a long time. Whichever technique works to get you mentally ready is, of course, the one you should use.

A high level of self-confidence is necessary for successful competition. If your level of confidence is already high enough, without being overly confident, you may need little more than to keep thinking positive thoughts. If your confidence is not at your optimum level, take time to boost it before competition. Thinking positive thoughts and reviewing successful past performance should both lead to increased confidence.

Some degree of physical activity may be very useful for psyching yourself up. Physical activity should relax the muscles, and the increased flow of oxygen to all parts of the body may be just what you need to prepare for competition.

It is NOT desirable to "hype yourself up" to the point that you are unnecessarily anxious about the situation. Keep in mind: an optimum level of beneficial anxiety should lead to maximum performance. Tension and anxiety are beneficial when you are still thinking positive thoughts. They become detrimental only when you begin to think negative thoughts. Find your optimum anxiety level.

You may have other ways of psyching yourself up for competition, since it is an individual matter. Whatever works best for you is good. Locate the mental techniques for preparing for competition, and incorporate them into your mental game.

PSYCHING YOURSELF DOWN is a concept that is not given sufficient thought by many bowlers or other athletes. There are two instances when psyching yourself down has validity and usefulness. It is very important to know how to deal with these two situations.

The first instance is when you are already "too keyed up", your anxiety and tension levels are above your optimum range. At such times you have to find ways to "de-excite" yourself, to calm down.

The second case where psyching yourself down is very beneficial to good mental health occurs when you have suffered a defeat,--- you have failed in some competition. In bowling, most people will NOT win more often than they WILL win.

First, let's look at the situation where you are overly excited, and need to calm your thoughts. Two instances where this may occur are when you have just won a major victory, or when you are preparing to enter a major competition.

In a highly excited state, prior to an important match or tournament, the mind is in a state of disorder. De-excitation, or a cooling and calming down process, tends to produce a more orderly state of mind, putting you back in control of your thoughts.

Some professional bowling finalists relax themselves while waiting for their turn to bowl in the television finals by watching the show on the monitors. This tends to relax them and take their mind off the wait. Others prefer to be on the practice lanes, working out excess tension, and distracting themselves from negative thoughts that might occur while they wait.

Meditation, relaxation, and other calming techniques are some of the best ways to handle the instances where you are too keyed up prior to competition. These are discussed in Section 9, RELAXATION, and therefore will not be repeated here. It is, however, worthwhile to mention a few words about bringing yourself down to reality after a WIN.

For some people, learning how to take a win is more difficult than learning how to accept a loss. Many potentially good athletes have become has-beens because they were not able to gracefully and humbly let themselves down from the lofty heights of exhilaration often associated with a win.

It is important to take winning in stride, and not let it get out of perspective. Everyone has heard of athletes who had success come quickly, and who were not able to put the win into proper perspective. Their inflated sense of importance, and their over-estimate of their abilities led them to distraction. They lost sight of their objectives and expected success to follow every try. They became impatient with themselves, expected too much from themselves, and in general lost control of their mental game.

Their inflated image of themselves, not in proper perspective, alienated them from others. This isolation, combined with an over-emphasis upon winning, contributed to mental and physical deterioration. Further wins became more difficult, thus creating a vicious cycle that led to decay in both the mental and physical games. They were, in effect, ruined by success.

The second situation calling for "psyching yourself down" occurs after you have suffered a defeat, or have not achieved your goal in some competitive situation. For bowlers (like golfers, but unlike major tennis stars) not winning will occur much more frequently than winning. Therefore it becomes very important to know how to deal with such non-winning situations. You must not let failure to win diminish your mental skills, so that your mental outlook is not up to par for your next competitive situation. You must not "get down" on yourself.

When you make a mistake, execute a bad shot, lose an important match, etc., don't lose confidence in yourself. If you err, accept it. Sure, you could have done better; but why let one mistake create another one? Accept the mistake and go on to the next competition. Getting down on yourself will create a formidable opponent: yourself! You are the most powerful friend or powerful enemy you have. Why have to beat yourself and your opponents?

"Mental or psychological scars" can develop after an unsuccessful performance, or a series of unsuccessful competitions. This can have a detrimental impact on your mental game. How you handle your failures can either be a growth experience preparing you for future success, or lead in the direction of further failure. You should develop an attitude that makes competitive situations growth experiences, opportunities for strengthening your mental game.

One way to avoid a letdown after a failure is to know that you have performed as well as you could, and to accept whatever happens. Wins and losses are both integral parts of competition. Try to learn from your losses as well as from your wins. It is fine to reflect back on your performance during the competition, but do not dwell on it. (Shortly I will illustrate how dwelling on a previous loss cost one bowler about $15,000 in a little more than one hour.)

One of the teachings of judo is to learn how to fall. This concept also relates to the mental games of bowling, golf, tennis, and any other competitive activity.

In judo, the fall is a physical one. You learn how to fall in a relaxed manner that prevents physical injury. The fall in bowling is a mental fall. You must learn how to "fall" from a disappointment, a loss, a run of bad luck, in such a way that you prevent mental injuries. Mentally letting yourself down gracefully is learning how to fall mentally.

Anytime something does not go well for you, there is the possibility of "falling mentally" and injuring yourself mentally. Being aware of this concept, borrowed from the art of judo, should alert you to the need for gracefully accepting your losing situations.

Post-competitive attitudes and emotions can have either a beneficial or detrimental effect on your mental game as you enter subsequent competitions. Over the long run, a negative attitude after an unsuccessful competition can develop into a totally negative mental game. This reduces your chances for future success.

Try to find something positive about your performances even in unsuccessful competitions. Judge yourself not so much on the result, but upon the effort you put forth. As long as you have given your best effort, the competition should be viewed as successful. This attitude following competition can develop into a healthy mental game, that will improve your chances for future success.

An opportunity to practice falling gracefully occurs frequently. This happens when you get an apparently perfect pocket hit and leave the 8 or 9-pin. I suggested elsewhere that you "salute the pin", instead of cussing at it. Look at the pin as a worthy opponent who has stood up to your best shot. Congratulate the pin. Salute it! After all, there is no way you can change the result, so why not use the opportunity to practice graceful falling? In the long run, a positive mental attitude to such events will lead to better mental growth, and to a more stable, relaxed attitude.

In closing this section on psyching yourself down, I would like to relate a story of a bowler who dwelt so much on one loss that it probably cost him over $15,000 in about an hour. This happened at the High Rollers Tournament in Las Vegas.

This bowler reached the final eight contestants in the High Rollers Tournament, worth almost $1 million dollars. He lost his match, and then had to bowl to see if he would finish in 5th, 6th, 7th, or 8th place. The difference between 5th and 8th places was about $15,000. If he could win his next match, he would win about $16,000. If he could win his next two matches, he would win about $25,000. If he lost both matches he still won $10,000. Thus, a considerable amount of money was still to be earned if he could perform well.

It was obvious from watching him that his mind was not on his current match; it was still on the last match he lost. He bowled almost 40 pins under his tournament average in his last two matches, lost both, and thereby lost his chance to win an extra $15,000. His inability to let himself down gracefully from a previous loss, to erase it from his mind, probably cost him $15,000 in additional prize money.

What he should have done was quickly put his previous loss out of his mind. There was nothing he could do about it. It was over. He should have let himself down gracefully (psychologically speaking), and put all his attention on the current match. If he had done this, I feel sure he would have won his final two matches, and the $15,000 difference between 5th and 8th place. His mental game lapse, in my opinion, cost him that much money in about an hour.

By way of a brief summary, I would like to recap the major concepts discussed in this section on psyching yourself up and down.

First, there is an optimum mental or psychological level of performance for each individual. In fact, there is a range in which your emotions and attitudes could fluctuate. When the emotions are too high, you need to take action to bring them back to a more normal level. When the emotions sink too low, you must raise them up to a more optimal level. These actions are called psyching yourself up and down.

Psyching yourself up does not necessarily mean keying yourself up. Psyching yourself up for competition means mentally preparing yourself to compete. Some people perform best when they are under some stress, while others perform best in a calm emotional state. You must know your ideal emotional level, and develop methods for achieving it.

The objective of psyching yourself up and down is to stabilize your range of emotions. Minor ups and downs will occur. As long as these minor fluctuations are within your normal range for performing well, they can be ignored.

It is important to develop the proper mental attitude for coping with both wins and losses. Both situations present the possibility for either mental growth or mental deterioration. Your attitude following each one determines its affect on your mental game.

Emotional control is one of the key ingredients in a good mental game. When you are at a low emotional level, you must find ways to psych yourself up. When you are overly excited, and the mind is in a state of disorder, you must learn how to produce a more orderly state of mind in which you remain in control. In short, you must take control of and responsibility for your emotions at all times.

Learn how to Psych Yourself Down.

How DO you hold
your free arm
during the swing?

When subconscious thoughts become
conscious, competence may be reduced.

--- PSYCHING OUT YOUR OPPONENT MEANS GETTING HIM OR HER OFF BALANCE, BOTH MENTALLY AND PHYSICALLY.---

When you psych yourself up or down, you are controlling your own emotions. When you try to psych out your opponent, you are attempting to control his or her emotions. Thus, the concept raises some interesting moral and ethical questions. Whether you intend to use psyching techniques or not, you should be aware of them in order to minimize any effect they might have on you.

Psyching-out the opponent is a term often heard at athletic events. It means: any attempt to disrupt the normal game of the opponent. The objective of a psych-job is usually to gain a psychological or mental edge or advantage over your opponent, by disrupting his mental or physical game.

Disrupting the normal game of your opponent means getting him or her off-balance, both mentally and physically. It means creating self-doubt, lack of confidence, or lack of desire. Psyching-out the opponent means disrupting the normal rhythm, pace, or pattern that he or she prefers. It means aggravating or agitating the opponent so that his or her mental game is not normal, which hopefully will be reflected in a physical game that is sub-par.

The authors of SPORTS PSYCHING (Tutko and Tosi) identify four areas into which all psyching methods can be classified:(1) PROVOCATION, or stirring the opponents up by giving them the cold shoulder, making comments to "rattle" them, or treating them in a condescending manner, as though you are the teacher and they are the student. (2) INTIMIDATION, trying to impress your opponents with your superiority, or implying that you know something they do not know (what equipment or strike line to use). (3) EVOKING GUILT FEELINGS, by being too nice, playing the poor soul routine, or pretending that you don't really care about the competition. (4) DISTRACTION, by attracting attention with a tantrum, or praising them, implying that they are playing over their heads. Most psyching attempts could probably be placed into one of these four categories. (Incidentally, I highly recommend SPORTS PSYCHING, listed in the Bibliography.)

What are some specific ways bowlers try to psych-out their opponents? A few of these methods are: not watching when the opponent is bowling; re-racking as often as you are permitted to do; calling for a re-rack even when you know you will probably not be granted permission to do so; bowling at a slow pace when the opponent is known to prefer a fast pace; bowling at a fast pace when the opponent is known to prefer a slow pace; altering the pace of the game so the opponent is kept off balance and cannot find a good rhythm or pattern; pretending you are not interested in what is happening (acting nonchalant); acting as though the opponent is having good luck instead of bowling well; Etc.

Sometimes a "brooklyn" strike is enough to psych out your opponent. If it upsets your opponent, and you use psyching, you might deliberately try for an early brooklyn strike.

A psyching strategy of questionable merit that is often used in league play is to buy drinks for your opponents, before or during competition. I have seen league championships won and lost this way.

Sometimes talking or not talking to your opponent is used to gain an edge. Taking an aloof attitude, refusing to recognize or talk to your opponent, may distress him. He may think you are mad at him, want to know why, and become preoccupied with trying to find out what he may or may not have done to cause you to act this way. His mind wanders and his game suffers.

On the other hand, talking to an opponent may have a similar effect. You can deliberately plant ideas into his head which may or may not be correct, causing him to bowl at less than his true potential.

Of course there are many other methods for attempting to psych-out your opponents. The above are simply representative of the areas in which opportunities exist to disrupt their normal game. You might ask how high he or she takes the ball in the backswing; or what they do with their free hand during the delivery; or how close to the foul line their non-sliding foot stops. These and similar questions plant doubts in their minds, and cause them to consciously think about things which they would not normally be thinking about. This conscious attention to what should have been sub-conscious activities will often reduce the effectiveness of the opponent's delivery.

It is obvious from some of the above examples that many devious, crafty, sneaky or underhanded ways exist for disrupting your opponents. Since such possibilities exist, you must be aware of them for self-protection purposes, even if you never intend to use any psyching techniques.

A word of caution is in order at this time. Not all psyching situations are deliberate. Some actions are unintentional, although the effect might be the same. For example, many of the incidents described above (talking or not talking, getting a brooklyn strike, asking some question about the delivery, etc.) happen in an innocent manner, with no ulterior or psyching motive intended. The person doing such things may be innocent of any wrong intent, but may be showing a lack of judgment. Therefore, be cautious about accusing your opponent of using psyching techniques. He or she may be innocent of any wrong-doing.

To psych or not to psych: that is the question. Should attempts to psych-out the opponent be used? Are activities designed to reduce the effectiveness of your opponent legal? ethical? moral? And, if so, how often and when should they be used?

Such questions are difficult to answer and must be addressed on a personal and individual basis. Two extreme schools of thought exist on the subject. One group, in favor of psyching, feels that the use of such techniques is a normal and natural part of the mental game of bowling or any other competitive activity. Thus, they feel it is perfectly natural to use psyching-out techniques. They reason, quite logically, that the game is largely mental at the higher skill levels, and use of such mental techniques for gaining a mental or psychological advantage is justified.

Those who use psyching methods, study the mental and physical strengths and weaknesses of their opponents. The goal is to minimize the strengths of their opponents or to capitalize on their weaknesses. (Notice the amount of time those who use psyching spend thinking about their opponents, time which probably could be better spent thinking about their own game or strategy for winning.)

On the other hand, others feel that the game should be decided purely on the basis of technical skills; that the best person should be allowed to win; that each contestant should concentrate on his or her own game and not try to unduly influence the game of the opponent. They see psyching-out techniques as unsportsmanlike at best, and unethical at worst. They feel that any athlete who must resort to psyching is not confident in his or her ability to win with talent. This group reasons that the contest is on bowling skills, and the best person should win based on performance on the lanes.

There is obviously some merit to both points of view. Each extreme is reached by logical thinking, even though the two conclusions are exactly opposite. Both sides would probably agree that there are some actions designed to disrupt their opponent's game which would be classified as unacceptable. For example, threatening phone calls prior to competition would be very disruptive of performance, yet certainly not condoned by any concerned sportsperson. The question, therefore, becomes a personal one of deciding where you draw the line between what you will do, or will not do, to gain a competitive edge over your opponent.

Between the two extremes given above is a wide range of gray area. It is clear that the mental game is a significant aspect of high-level competition. Some mental strategies are necessary. The question is: what psyching strategies do you consider proper and ethical?

There is no definite answer I can give that would suit every person's mental approach to the game. You must find the answer which is consistent with your moral and ethical standards of sportsmanship. To help you make that decision, I will present ways to defend yourself against psyching techniques, so you will have a chance to see both sides of the situation: how to psych and how to defend against it.

Before doing that, let's look at how psyching-out your opponents may disrupt their game, but this disruption may not be to your advantage. Two things may happen that could put you (not your opponent) at a disadvantage: (1) You might spend so much time, energy, and effort trying to psych-out your opponent that your own game suffers, or (2) you may arouse your opponent to the point that he or she performs better, not worse!

Some people perform best when they have been aroused or agitated. They rise to the occasion and are able to out-do themselves when they have been the subject of an attempted psych-job. They want to react to the attempt at disruption with a vengeance, seeking revenge for what they feel are unsportsmanlike activities.

And now a look at psyching defenses. What is your best defense against psyching tactics? Perhaps the best defense is control of your emotions and confidence in your own game.

Assuming an air of confidence may be distressing to your competitors. Winners exude confidence. They radiate a feeling that they are invincible; they cannot be beaten; nothing can upset their game. They think, act, feel, talk, and bowl like they can do no wrong. This is often upsetting to the opponent, who may subconsciously resign himself to defeat, or try so hard that it reduces his level of performance.

Therefore, assuming an air of invincibility can be used either as a defense against psyching or as a psyching technique itself.

Ignoring their tactics and maintaining a firm CONCENTRATION on the task at hand will minimize any psyching efforts. In effect, you are psyching-yourself-IN while they are trying to psych you OUT.

Ignoring psyching attempts may even have an adverse effect on the one trying to perpetrate the psych job. He may get frustrated because you are not being bothered by his methods of diversion. He may spend so much time trying to bother you that his own game suffers. Ignoring the "psycher" seems to offer a good defense against psyching techniques.

In conclusion, if you are going to use psyching-out techniques you must know your opponents and how they normally react to such efforts. Some competitors can be psyched-out. Others react in the opposite manner, as indicated above. You can psych yourself out if you are not careful.

Even if you are not going to use psyching techniques, at least become aware of the more common methods being used so you can take defensive actions to prevent them from adversely affecting your game.

Defending yourself against psyching techniques is a valuable competitive weapon to have in your mental game arsenal. You may not be able to avoid those who try to psych their opponents, but you can minimize or eliminate their impact upon you.

That's right! I'm not shaving until I break this slump.

--- A SLUMP CAN BE A HUMBLING EXPERIENCE. YOU CAN COME OUT OF IT A BETTER PERSON. ---

Athletes of all types eventually face a prolonged period of time in which their performance is far below normal for them. These periods of sub-par performance are called slumps. They appear to be a natural and normal part of every sporting activity. Bowling is no exception. Bowlers encounter slumps which may last only a few days, but could last for a year or more. (Marshall Holman's TV slump lasted almost two years! He made the show almost 20 times, but could not win a title.)

Although the existence of slumps is well accepted, any explanation of the reasons for their existence is a complex matter. At the heart of the subject is the vast difference in physical and mental makeup of all athletes. What may cause one bowler to go into a slump may have no such effect on another person. What will bring one bowler out of a slump may not work at all for another bowler.

Since there is no single cause for slumps, there is no single cure for them. I will try to describe methods which can lead you to find a cure which works for you. Since slumps cannot be entirely eliminated, the best you can hope for is to minimize the impact they have on your performance. Your skill development efforts will be hampered if you are not able to handle slumps promptly and properly.

TYPES OF SLUMPS: Slumps may be either mentally or physically based. You can PLAY YOURSELF INTO A SLUMP by allowing a fault to develop in your physical game, or THINK YOURSELF INTO A MENTAL SLUMP by allowing a mental fault to enter into your mental game. Both types of slumps result in below-average performance for a sustained period of time.

The existence of two types of slumps creates a situation where a vicious cycle could develop. A physical slump could cause a mental slump, and vice versa. For example, if you let a fault creep into your physical game, causing you to perform poorly, then your mental attitude could deteriorate. On the other hand, you could develop a poor mental attitude which adversely affects your physical game. Poor physical performance (the approach and delivery) and poor mental performance (improper attitude, incorrect thinking, lack of confidence, etc.) can combine to produce a difficult cycle to break.

To end a slump you may need to know whether it has a mental or physical base. This may be difficult to determine since an element of both may have caused the slump. To end a physical slump you need to get back to basics and locate the physical fault. Then you can work the fault out of your game. To end a mental slump requires a change in attitude, thinking or confidence. This is easy to say but difficult to do. A mental slump may be far more difficult to locate and correct than one which has a physical basis.

CAUSES FOR SLUMPS: Some of the specific causes for slumps include: lack of confidence; either failure to concentrate or concentrating too hard; stress, tension or fatigue resulting from bowling too much; carelessness, problems with timing in the approach and delivery; other delivery faults; and personal problems. These are only a few causes for performing below your average level for a long time period.

It is possible to develop mental fatigue, just as readily as it is to develop physical fatigue. One refers to a weakness of the body, while the other one refers to a weakness of the mind. The latter is often referred to as "getting stale", often resulting in a slump. When you feel mental fatigue coming on, tend to it just as quickly as you would to physical fatigue. Often all that is needed is to focus your attentions on something other than bowling, to not bowl for a week or a month or longer.

Still another reason why slumps occur relates to the conscious and subconscious mind. It could be that the conscious mind does not trust the subconscious mind. You begin consciously thinking about all parts of the delivery. You do not trust the body to perform the delivery in an automatic manner. You try to take conscious control over what were previously subconscious movements and actions, reverting back to either CONSCIOUS COMPETENCE or CONSCIOUS INCOMPETENCE. (See Section 3).

To illustrate the effect of reverting to a prior stage in skill development, try typing, but look at every key as you did when you were learning. Speed and accuracy suffer. A skill such as typing can only be executed automatically, subconsciously.

The above situation is similar to a pressure situation. The bowler tries too hard to make an exceptionally good shot, instead of trying for a normal, automatic delivery of the ball. The conscious mind does not trust the subconscious mind to perform well.

STOPPING A SLUMP: How do you break out of a mental or physical slump? Advice often heard is to forget the slump and it will go away. As with all cures, this one works for some bowlers and not for others. Such advice is consistent with the belief that consciously thinking about something causes it to happen. The more pre-occupied you are with your slump, the more you may prolong it.

Consciously thinking about negative events often causes them to happen. Thinking about positive things will also cause them to happen. Our thoughts are often translated into deeds by our bodies. This concept is referred to as a self-fulfilling tendency of the body. How often have you left the 10-pin and worried so much about missing it that you actually did miss it? Thinking negative thoughts causes negative actions to happen.

Thinking positive thoughts causes positive actions to happen. Forget about the slump, relegate it to your subconscious mind, and it may go away as naturally as it came.

Still others feel that the only way out of a slump is to work your way out of it. This method works for some people but not for others, due to the individualistic nature of sports performances. Working your way out of a slump may mean a great deal of practice. It may also mean a return to the basics, taking your game apart and putting it back together again. The degree to which you are SENSITIVE AND AWARE of your entire game will determine how effective this method will be toward ending a slump. (See Section 4, SENSITIVITY AND AWARENESS.)

Some bowlers try more practice to work out of the slump. If this does not work, they stop bowling for a period of time. How can such diverse approaches to the slump situation work? Simply because what works for one person may not work for another. This PRINCIPLE OF DIVERSITY should be kept in mind when someone tells you there is only one way to end your slump. That way, whatever it is, may work for that person but it may have no effect on you.

The return-to-basics method for curing a slump has many advocates. And it does work for many people. This is particularly true if you have a physical problem or fault that has entered your delivery. Such bowlers begin to consciously think about all aspects of the approach and delivery. Others focus on one key aspect, the feel of the fingers at release, feel of the swing, feel of extension, etc. They do this temporarily, only to try to locate the source of the problem. Reverting back to conscious competence is one way to locate and correct faults in either your physical or mental game.

Here is where it is helpful to have someone who knows your game assist you in the search for the problem. It is not easy to see what you are doing incorrectly. A subtle fault can develop so gradually that it feels natural to you. A coach, instructor, or good friend who knows your game and the fundamentals of bowling, can be very helpful when you use this deliberate, conscious approach to find the sources of your slump.

Your normal way of bowling should be subconscious and automatic. You have trained the muscles to do certain things with no deliberate thought on your part. If you are in a slump and are trying to get out of it by concentrating on your delivery, you are deliberately not bowling in your normal manner. This makes it difficult to locate your problem, and suggests the need for an outsider to locate it. Even top bowlers recognize the need for a coach or instructor to locate minute changes in their normal game.

In summary, accept both mental and physical slumps as a normal part of bowling. If you keep yourself in good mental and physical condition, keep your physical and mental games intact, then any slumps that you might have should be very short-lived. Know your game so well that you can take it apart and put it back together again when a fault has developed.

Develop a sensitivity and awareness to all aspects of your game. Try to maintain your confidence and a positive outlook. The mind is powerful. It controls the body. When both your mental and physical games are strong, slumps will not present any problem for you.

Buying a new ball often gives you a big psychological lift.

Learn how to control your temper,
so your temper won't control you.

--- A FAULT IS AN OPPORTUNITY TO LEARN, NOT A PERSONAL FAILING. ---

Mental faults can be conveniently grouped into two categories for analysis: KNOWLEDGE faults and ATTITUDE faults. This section discusses attitude faults and the following one concerns knowledge faults. Both types of mental problems need to be eliminated if a sound mental game is to be achieved.

What is a mental fault? Although the answer to this question may seem obvious to most bowlers, it is not as obvious as one would think.

A dictionary might define a FAULT as a failing, transgression, defect, impairment, mistake or sin. Implied in each of these definitions is the idea that a fault is something which does not measure up to some standard. A fault is something undesirable and in need of correction.

I prefer to define a MENTAL FAULT in this manner: any permanent part of your mental game which prevents you from achieving a higher average than you currently have, or which prevents you from having more success with your bowling. Viewed in this manner, a mental fault is any way you think, or do not think, that prevents you from having a higher average than you now have.

The above definition means there is some change you can make in your ATTITUDE about bowling or KNOWLEDGE about the game which will have a beneficial and positive effect on your ability to score well on a consistent, long term basis. A fault, thus defined, is an opportunity for improvement.

This definition uses IMPACT ON AVERAGE as the standard to assess any part of your mental or physical game. Your average is the best means of judging your performance. If you are bowling well, are executing your shots well, then you will be scoring well and will achieve a high average.

Another aspect of this definition focuses on the permanent nature of the fault. A fault is a PERMANENT part of your mental game. A fault is SOMETHING YOU DO on a regular basis, or SOME WAY YOU THINK on a regular basis. A fault may be something you DO NOT DO or SOMETHING YOU DO NOT think about. There can be faults created by sins of OMISSION (not doing something), or by sins of COMMISSION (doing something, but doing it incorrectly).

Every bowler makes an occasional mental mistake or error in thinking. No bowler thinks perfectly every time he or she is bowling. It is the FREQUENCY OF OCCURRENCE that determines whether a fault exists. If your attitude is normally INcorrect, and if it continues to prevent you from achieving your maximum potential average, then it is a permanent fault and must be corrected.

The permanent nature of an attitude fault, according to my definition, means that anyone who attempts to assist you must observe you for a sufficient time to know how you think on a regular basis. Of course, a skilled instructor may be able to detect permanent faults very quickly.

Notice: the definition of a fault makes no reference to how you think compared to any other person. THE AVERAGE IS THE JUDGE. Any part of your attitude toward bowling that keeps your average lower than it could be, is an attitude fault that needs correction.

Strictly interpreted, the definition means that everybody has faults in their mental game. Everybody could improve their average until they reach a perfect 300 average. Is it possible to have faults if you are averaging 240?

Obviously anyone who averages 120 is lacking in both physical and mental parts of their game (unless that person is extremely young, extremely old, physically or mentally handicapped, or has other extenuating circumstances which would make this a very high average for them). Someone who is legitimately averaging 240, on the other hand, cannot be doing too many things incorrectly, and must be doing just about everything correctly. Even a perfect delivery every time will not guarantee you a strike in every frame. Many factors could cause you to get less than a strike on what appears to be a perfect (faultless) delivery of the ball.

Each person has a maximum attainable average for him or her. That maximum could be an average of 160 or lower, 180, 200, 220, or higher. The current season average record for women is 227 and for men it is 240. Thus, assuming you have no physical or mental impairments, these could be considered theoretical maximums. Until you have reached your maximum average, you have (in our definition) faults which are keeping you from reaching your full average potential. As long as your average can be improved, your mental or physical game can be improved.

Faults, when viewed properly, can be opportunities for improvement and not seen as personal failings. Consider yourself in the process of developing, and not having arrived at your maximum development level.

Attitude faults should be considered parts of your mental game that are in need of improvement.

Do not become disturbed when your faults are uncovered; be thankful. If you cannot uncover them you cannot correct them. If you cannot correct them, you cannot achieve your full average potential. Recognition and acceptance are essential to correction. Failure to accept the fact that you have faults assures that they will continue to keep your average lower than it could be, and will reduce your chances for high scores and winning performances.

Attitude faults are inconsistent with good bowling. They are preconceived ideas which are incorrect. In the remainder of this section we will discuss specific kinds of attitudes and emotions that prevent you from developing a sound mental game.

Your emotional state can be a source of errors and faults in your delivery. You could be over-eager, and your enthusiasm could cause you to rush the foul line, to throw (instead of roll) the ball, to raise up at the foul line, etc. Do not let your emotional state create problems. Try to remain in control of your emotions while you are on the approach and until the ball is on its way to the pins. Then, if you have to, you can release your emotions. Control your emotions and you control this source of mental problems.

Another mental fault related to attitudes and emotions, concerns how you normally react to pressure situations. Some bowlers must fight themselves to win when the situation is tense. Their opponents don't have to do anything to beat them. They beat themselves, by bowling much lower than their averages. Such people, in my opinion, have mental faults which stand in the way of reaching their full potential.

A major attitude problem concerns those who consider bowling as nothing but a physical game with little or no mental content. This might be the biggest mental fault, because those who have such an attitude are not capable of learning much about the sport. They do not realize how much they do not know, nor do they realize how much one needs to know to bowl well. With such an attitude, they are not very receptive to any information about the game. They think they know all they need to know to bowl well. (More on this in the following section.)

It is easy to see how so many people have such an INcorrect attitude. Bowling is often promoted as a "nothing activity": you DO NOT need any equipment; you DO NOT need any shoes; you DO NOT need any special physical strengths or skills; you DO NOT need to be any age, etc.

This negative type of advertising and promotion has caused many bowlers to think that they know all about bowling when they can roll the ball down the lane. There is a great deal of difference between rolling a ball down a lane and good bowling. That distinction needs to be understood by those who have this incorrect attitude.

Closely related to the "nothing attitude" is the attitude held by many bowlers that you cannot learn how to bowl except by bowling. This attitude is no doubt fostered by those who want to develop open-play and practice lineage.

"You can't learn how to bowl by reading a book", is an incorrect statement commonly heard. The false implication from this statement is that there is nothing to learn about bowling; one must simply get on the lanes and practice to develop bowling skills to their full potential. Nothing could be further from the truth. You can learn WHAT you have to do from well-written books, or coaches and instructors. You must get on the lanes to learn HOW to put what you know into practice. Both the WHAT and HOW are necessary for skill development.

Yet another attitude fault is one displayed by bowlers who confuse the simplicity of the goal with the complexity of achieving that goal. The objective of bowling is very simple: knock down all ten pins with the first ball for a strike. If you fail to do this, you must knock down the remainder with the second ball for a spare.

EXPLAINING the objective of almost any sport is normally a simple matter: scoring a bullseye in archery; a touchdown in football; a basket in basketball; or using the least number of strokes in golf; etc. ACHIEVING the objective is the complexity of the sport.

It is possible, in any given frame, to score a perfect strike while doing nothing correctly. Each such strike reinforces this simplistic attitude if only for the moment. In effect, the game is its own worse enemy when it permits perfection (a strike) from the most non-perfect executions. If skill were needed to get even one strike, the complexities of the game would be more obvious. (Yet bowling would probably lose some of its universal appeal.)

There needs to be more focus on THE AVERAGE. The average is a far more accurate indicator of skill than the result of a single frame, game or series which could have been achieved largely due to luck. The complexity of bowling is not understood by those who have the attitude that good bowling is a simple activity, that anyone can bowl well.

An always-or-never attitude is the source of another major mental fault which tends to prevent skill development in many bowlers: "I ALWAYS use the second arrow for all my strike deliveries". "I have ALWAYS bowled that way". "I NEVER have used spot bowling". "I NEVER read any books on bowling". (A bowling coach BOASTED to me that he had NEVER read ANY bowling book. Imagine keeping all written knowledge of bowling from yourself and your students, and claiming you are qualified to teach bowling!)

Such ALWAYS and NEVER statements are used by bowlers who are unnecessarily restricting the development of their potential on the lanes. There are too many variables in bowling to "always or never" do anything. Even major principles of bowling should be violated on occasion.

Closely related to the above is the UNwillingness of some bowlers to admit their shortcomings, their faults. As I previously stated, RECOGNITION OF A PROBLEM IS THE FIRST STEP TOWARD A SOLUTION. Until a fault is recognized and accepted as a problem, no effort will be made to find a solution for it.

This section has only covered a few of the attitudes and emotions which we call mental faults. Others include lack of concentration, poor sportsmanship habits, a negative or defeatist attitude, etc. These additional mental faults are discussed in other sections, throughout this book.

If you are to achieve your full potential, the HIGHEST AVERAGE of which you are capable, you will have to eliminate attitude-related mental faults. Now that you are aware of them, you can begin to remove them from your mental game.

THE LEAGUE'S
MOST IMPROVED
BOWLER AWARD

Learn WHAT to do by reading books.
Learn HOW to do it on the lanes.

--- THE MOST PREVALENT KNOWLEDGE FAULT IS THE BELIEF THAT YOU ALREADY KNOW ALL YOU NEED TO KNOW. ---

High-average bowling requires the acquisition of KNOWLEDGE that can be used to develop an effective delivery, and a positive and constructive ATTITUDE towards bowling in general and competitive bowling in particular. Faulty thinking can become a part of both areas of the mental game. The previous section discussed mental faults related to attitudes. This section will continue the area of mental faults by looking at KNOWLEDGE FAULTS.

The deceptively simple nature of bowling belies what knowledge you must have to bowl well on a consistent basis. As previously stated, most bowlers have the mistaken belief that there is very little to learn about bowling once they are able to roll the ball down the lane. This is perhaps the most prevalent knowledge fault: the feeling among bowlers that they already have the requisite knowledge to bowl well; there is nothing more they need to know.

Knowledge about bowling can be grouped into four categories, reflecting the four key elements of the game. First is knowledge of the DELIVERY, which is the only thing a bowler does (deliver the ball). Second is information related to making STRIKES, the objective in every frame. Third are facts and data related to making SPARES when the strike effort was unsuccessful. And fourth, are all aspects of the MENTAL GAME, the subject of this book.

It is no accident that the first three categories represent the topics presented in the three volumes of THE ENCYCLOPEDIA OF BOWLING INSTRUCTION (written by George Allen and Dick Ritger), nor that the fourth area is the subject of this book. Lack of correct information in these four areas is the cause of mental bowling skills which are below what each bowler could achieve. Anyone interested in developing his or her bowling skills to the maximum must learn a great deal about (a) the delivery, (b) making strikes, (c) making spares, and (4) the mental game. Bowling additional lines may be helpful to your overall game. But the only practice that can be really meaningful is that which is directed toward achieving some specific objectives, toward learning what it is you need to know to bowl well.

Knowledge of the DELIVERY includes principles about both the physical and mental games. These principles cover such topics as: ball roll patterns (hook, curve, backup and straight ball); principles of aiming; principles of timing, consistency and naturalness; sportsmanship principles and principles related to all physical parts of the delivery (stance, pushaway, swing, steps, slide, release, follow through, etc.).

A consistent, natural and well-timed delivery can only be developed when you have gained knowledge in these areas. (These topics are covered in a separate Volume 1, THE COMPLETE GUIDE TO BOWLING PRINCIPLES.)

Principles of making STRIKES include knowledge in three areas. First is the general information on the requirements for the perfect strike hit, and the pocket speed, angle and action necessary for consistent strikes. Second is the broad area of reading the reaction of the ball surface with the lane surface. And third is the three types of adjustments required to properly play any lane condition: angle adjustments (including the five strike lines); equipment adjustments (including ball surfaces, balances and fits); and delivery adjustments (such as speed, lift and loft). Making strikes consistently (50% of the time) requires specific knowledge in these three areas. These topics are covered in Volume 2, THE COMPLETE GUIDE TO BOWLING STRIKES.

Required knowledge for successful SPARE conversions includes such topics as: key pin and contact points; cross lane angles; pin and ball deflection on spares; chops, speed, and splits as related to spares; the 14 Spare Zones; adjusting for lane conditions; and mathematical spare adjustment systems. These topics should be related to the 249 different spares you may have to make at one time or another in your bowling career. Making spares consistently (95% of the time) requires specific knowledge in these areas. These topics are covered in Volume 3, THE COMPLETE GUIDE TO BOWLING SPARES.

The knowledge side of the MENTAL GAME is obviously far more important than most bowlers realize. This is especially true at the higher average levels, where the total mental game (knowledge, attitudes, emotions and the topics included in this book) is far more important than the physical game (the approach and delivery). Most experts estimate that the mental game accounts for about 90% of the success of high-average bowlers. (See an illustration of this concept on the outside back cover.)

Mental faults concerning lack of or incorrect knowledge can be corrected in much the same way that physical faults are corrected. What is necessary is more information, correct information, and time spent on the lanes to develop the skill to put this information to use. You can get this information from well-written books or good coaching and instruction. The series of books---THE ENCYCLOPEDIA OF BOWLING INSTRUCTION---is a step in the direction of eliminating knowledge faults from the mental and physical games of serious bowlers. (The BIBLIOGRAPHY has a list of many books related to the mental game.)

Develop a list of your knowledge faults and try to place them into priority sequence. Perhaps when one fault is corrected, it will automatically correct another one. For example, the more information you gain about making strikes, the more often you will hit the pocket. The more often you hit the pocket, the higher your pin counts will be, resulting in easier spare leaves. Thus, your knowledge about making strikes has a direct impact on your spare making ability. If you attack your faults in a systematic and organized manner, you will make greater progress than if you go about eliminating them in a hit-or-miss, random manner.

Try to work on one fault at a time, and keep all else constant if you can. Take an entire practice session (or several sessions if necessary) and devote it exclusively to one particular fault. Keep in mind that you are trying to develop something that is going to last your entire bowling career. Build this foundation as carefully as you would build a brick wall, one piece at a time.

Expect any change that you make in your delivery, as a result of your new knowledge, to feel uncomfortable at first. Also expect your performance level to temporarily drop while you are working to correct the fault. It is an unusual bowler who can correct a fault and bowl at the same or a higher level during the time the altered delivery is being incorporated into his or her subconscious mind. That is why it is important to devote practice sessions to fault correction, when the score is not important.

Look for the basic problem instead of treating symptoms. Faults often have many sources, and there are usually many ways to correct a given fault. Analyze your complete approach and delivery fully, getting help from a qualified person if necessary before you conclude that you have located the actual fault. Be wary of coaches or so-called Self Appointed Bowling Instructors who are too quick to identify your so-called faults, and who tell you there is only one way to correct them. Many people have good intentions, and mean well, but they don't have sufficient knowledge to instruct others. They often do more harm than good, despite their intentions.

If you need assistance, seek the help of a qualified and trusted person when you have difficulty locating and correcting faults. Good instructors are hard to find, but are often very important in skill development. Don't be afraid to ask for help if you need it. Your ego can stand in the way of your progress. A natural, well-timed and consistent delivery is largely performed on a subconscious level. This makes it very difficult for the person to identify and isolate deviations in performance. Another person taking an objective look can be very helpful in locating faults.

Check your progress from time to time. Improvement should be reflected in your average, although this may not happen for some time. Don't be impatient. Set realistic time periods for progress, sometimes as little as a week or as long as a month or more. How often you practice, how well you practice, and the nature of the problem, will determine how soon you should reasonably expect an improvement in performance.

Once a particular knowledge fault is corrected, it should be gone from your game forever. It is not possible, however, to correct all your knowledge faults. LEARNING IS A NEVER-ENDING PROCESS, and you will never be able to know everything there is to know about every aspect of bowling. All you can reasonably hope for is continued progress and improved knowledge.

Once your major knowledge faults are eliminated, you should have a mental and physical game that will reward you with high-average performance for your entire bowling career. And, that is the ultimate objective of knowledge acquisition and skill development: high level performance on a regular and consistent basis for as long as you bowl.

Good physical health leads to good mental health.

Positive thoughts bring positive results.

--- WE BECOME WHAT WE THINK ABOUT ALL DAY LONG. ---

When the author attended the Professional Bowlers Association School, one instructor made a presentation based upon one sentence: "We become what we think about all day long." The body has a self-fulfilling capability, that is, the body tends to make what we think about come true. It is this capability of the mind, more specifically, the power of the imagination, which is the basis for this section.

This self-fulfilling tendency has enormous implications. We will explore a few of the specific ways you can harness your imagination, and use this tendency of the body to try to make happen what our imagination dwells upon.

In Section 18, A WINNING MENTAL GAME, a positive self-image is put forth as perhaps the most important aspect of a strong mental game. Your ability to think of yourself as a winner will largely determine whether you are able to become a winner. If you can visualize yourself as a winner, the self-fulfilling prophesy will be working in your favor. What you can imagine, the body will try to produce. If you cannot visualize yourself as a winner, it is highly unlikely that you will win.

Gary Skidmore attributed his first PBA win to the ability to imagine that he had already won. "I talked to Ted Hannahs after the position round Monday night and he told me to imagine during the night that I had already won, and I did just that. I didn't get much sleep but I got to see the dream come true.", said Skidmore, as it was reported by PBA. Skidmore had to win four games on TV to secure the title.

A positive self-image prepares you for success. A negative self-image prepares you for failure. Since you have the choice either to imagine yourself as a winner or as a loser, why not choose the option that leads to success?

The power to imagine is a talent that you can develop. With a well-developed imagination, you can imagine so clearly that it is impossible to distinguish what you have IMAGINED from what you have really EXPERIENCED. The full implication of this statement is enormous. This means that you do not have to actually win to experience what a winner experiences. You can vividly imagine it before it happens, (as Gary Skidmore did) and the imagination can help the reality occur. (Keep in mind the self-fulfilling tendency of the body.)

The visualization process can be equated to an imaginary television picture. If you are able to visualize very well, then you can see a very clear picture on the screen. People who have developed the ability to vividly imagine, are capable of fine tuning the picture they see on their imaginary TV screen, just as easily as they can actually fine tune their real TV sets.

VISUALIZE YOURSELF BEING A WINNER. Visualize yourself having confidence in your abilities. Visualize yourself doing the thing you want to be able to do. Such MENTAL PRACTICE can go a long way toward helping you reach in reality what you have vividly imagined.

Roger Twist, a serious bowler from Phoenix, Arizona, has an unusual way to help himself toward a perfect 300 game. He plans to make a TV recording of himself making a perfect strike. He plans to tape twelve such strikes, piece them together into one game, and replay his imaginary 300 game many times. This will definitely help him imagine his perfect game.

Roger Twist is helping his WONDERFUL IMAGINATION. You can help your imagination along. You can improve the way you dress to look like a winner, if you do not already do so. You can change your eating habits, and eat like a winner. You can put your imagination to work in all your practice sessions, simulating situations that you might have to face during competition: pretending you need to strike out to win; pretending you need to double to catch your opponent, etc.

The body cannot distinguish between something that you have vividly imagined and something that really happened. Think about this statement. It means that you can fool yourself into thinking positive thoughts, cause the body to react as if something you want to happen has actually happened.

For example, if you want to practice the ability to think normally when you have a string of strikes, try a little 9-pin no-tap (all 9 counts are recorded as strikes). You should be able to develop long strings of strikes, and shoot big scores. You will be in the position of practicing what it feels like to step up to the approach with a long string of strikes. And, keep in mind, the mind does not distinguish between no-tap strikes and "real ones". You might even enter no-tap tournaments to get the practice of bowling with a long string of strikes, but under actual tournament conditions.

Bowling in 3-6-9 Tournaments can have the same impact on your mental game. This format gives you a strike in the 3rd, 6th, and 9th frames in each game. This gives you 6 chances to double each game (before and after each free strike) and should let you build strings of strikes. Your scores should be higher, which will also let you take big scores in stride. Once you are used to rolling them, even in no-tap and 3-6-9 tournaments, it is a little easier to achieve them without help. The body does not distinguish between "real" 250 games and those bowled under favorable circumstances. (Look what happened to the 4-minute mile once the psychological barrier was broken!)

This may seem like trying to deceive yourself into thinking that you are better than you actually are. In fact, that is just the type of mental attitude that you want to develop (within reason), to build your confidence. If you build up your confidence, if you begin to think (vividly imagine) that big games are attainable, if you can learn how to react to long strings of strikes in a normal manner, then you are definitely building your mental game. And that is the objective of this entire book.

One technique that I often use to control potential pressure, actually to prevent it from occurring, is to say before each shot: "There is nothing special about this shot". This is an attempt to produce a relaxed, "practice mentality", under competitive pressures. To the extent that I am able to convince myself (fool myself) that there really is nothing special about each shot, I should be able to make my normal delivery under all circumstances.

If you are on 8-in-a-row, and begin thinking about that string of strikes, you give too much importance to the next shot, and try to consciously and deliberately do what you should be doing subconsciously. But, if you can fool your mind into thinking that there really is nothing special about the shot, you can prevent pressure from interfering with your normal delivery. As with all goals, this one may not be reached completely, but you should feel less pressure and be more relaxed when you are "working on a string of strikes".

Fooling the mind is just another way of saying that you are exercising mental control, you are imagining. You are controlling how the mind thinks by using visualization or imagination techniques.

For those of you who prefer pressure, who bowl better under pressure, you can change the sentence to: "There is something very special about this shot". In this way you can imagine that every shot is very special (which is true), and you could psych yourself up to better performances.

It is a true but disturbing fact that our imagination limits our potential. Your imagination can either set you free to achieve great goals, or make it highly unlikely that you will ever reach success. We create roadblocks to our achievements. It is all a matter of whether we imagine ourselves as full of self-doubt or full of self-confidence. Self-doubt will create psychological obstacles to performance. Self-confidence removes such barriers.

The concept of goals leads to still another fascinating aspect of our minds and imaginations. Goals often CREATE the energy and desire to achieve them. That is, if you set goals for yourself (if you imagine them clearly), and you want to achieve them, the body somehow generates the energy and enthusiasm to reach them. Perhaps this is another aspect of the self-fulfilling tendency of the body.

Have you ever felt tired, with nothing to do, and then got an idea that you wanted to put into effect? Having that goal, having something that you wanted to do, is somehow transformed by your body into the energy to reach it. This means that you can harness your imagination to set performance goals, and by doing this you will find the source of energy to reach these goals.

In conclusion, the ability to imagine is a wonderful asset. Your imagination sets the limits for your achievements. You become what you think about. If you think positive thoughts, set goals, the body will somehow generate the energy to help you reach those goals.

If you think you can do something, you probably will do it. If you think you can't do it you probably won't. Your imagination, your mind, can either be a potent enemy or a powerful friend. Isn't it time to get your wonderful imagination working for you? (You may wish to read the poem on the inside of the front cover, for inspiration and a source of positive thoughts.)

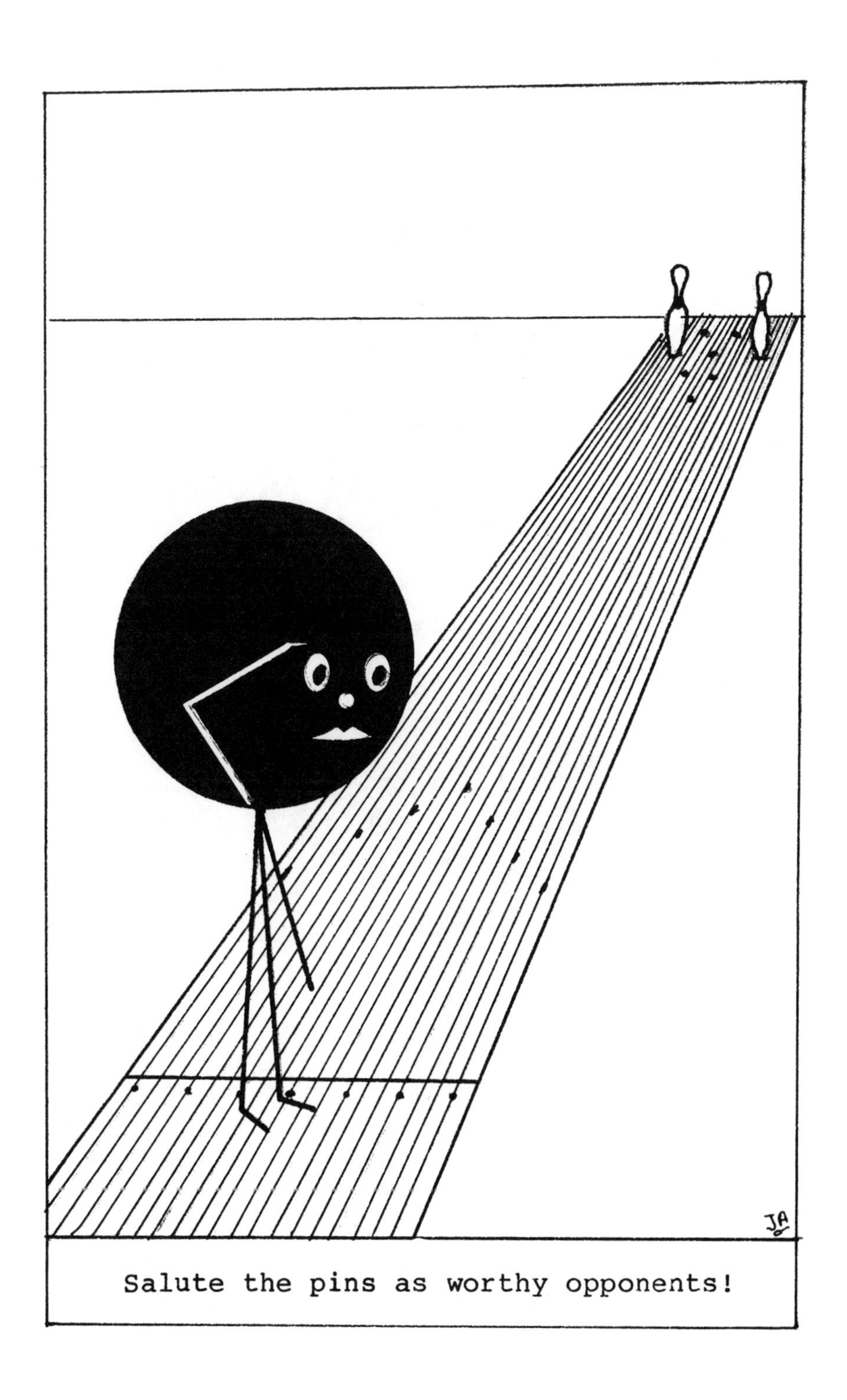

Salute the pins as worthy opponents!

Winning may create situations that are not altogether pleasant.

--- THE FEAR OF SUCCESS IS UNIVERSAL, SO WIDESPREAD THAT IT MUST BE CONSIDERED NORMAL ---, DR. Leon Tec.

A champion has been described as someone who has not only overcome the fear of losing but who has overcome the fear of winning as well. A true winner is not afraid of losing, but is not afraid of winning either.

Dr. Leon Tec, author of a book called THE FEAR OF SUCCESS, believes that "the fear of success is universal, so widespread that it must be considered normal". It seems strange to think that some people might be as afraid of success as they are of failure. Yet this is exactly what is implied in the concept of the FEAR OF SUCCESS.

Perhaps the fear of success IS a universal concept. At least it is probably more widespread than people would like to admit. After all, admitting that you are afraid of success seems almost sacrilegious in the United States, where competitive sports is such a prominent part of daily activities. Success is almost a religion in this country, and anyone who admitted that he or she was afraid of winning would certainly be looked upon with some degree of suspicion. That is why the fear of success, when it afflicts someone, is largely a subconscious psychological block. Few people would openly admit that they did not want to succeed at anything, or that they were afraid of winning.

17-158 THE FEAR OF SUCCESS

SUCCESS COMES AT A PRICE. Most people make the assumption that success is worth the cost. Normally, this is true. Yet there are times when the price of success is far more than a person is willing to pay. It is in these cases, when the price seems too high to pay for success, that the fear of success comes into play.

Perhaps it might be worthwhile to make a distinction between the fear of success and the fear of failure, since the two are opposites. The fear of failure is usually a conscious concern that you do not have the competence to win. You would like to win, and are not afraid of winning, but you do not think you have whatever skills are required to win. This fear of failure may be based upon solid facts (you know your limitations), or it may be unfounded. It could simply be a lack of confidence in your own abilities.

The fear of success, on the other hand, is usually a subconscious concern about winning, a fear that if you succeed the gains will not outweigh the losses. You may actually want to win, but subconscious thoughts may be creating doubts and adversely affecting your performances and chances of winning.

The fear of success represents a threat to the psychological health of the individual. Because it is based in the subconscious mind, its effect is perhaps more potent, and it is very difficult to recognize when the condition exists.

It is difficult to correct a situation that is hard to understand, recognize, and accept. The fear of failure, on the other hand, is at a more conscious level; you are more aware of it. This conscious awareness makes it easier to accept and to correct.

The fear of success and the desire to win can co-exist; they can be held in the mind at the same time. Sometimes there is an internal mental struggle between these two thought processes. You can have a conscious desire to win and a sub-conscious fear of success as well.

The desire to win is probably held in the minds of all competitors, to some extent or other. Most people who enter into competitive situations do so with the hope or expectation of winning. Therefore, do not dismiss the fear of success as a concept that does not apply to you, simply because you feel so strongly that you want to win. The psychological basis for the fear is too real to be dismissed lightly. It must be addressed as a possible mental problem to be overcome, if your mental game is to be as healthy as it can be.

The fear of success is a real fear. Although the fear has a strong subconscious base, it is not an imaginary fear. Since this type of mental problem does exist, and has a subconscious base, it is important that you recognize its existence and look for its symptoms. You are probably not affected by it, but you will never know for sure until you understand the concept. Besides, even if you have no problems with the fear of success, someone you care about could have such a fear and you could help them immeasurably. As with all mental faults, it should be identified, isolated, and a plan of action formulated to correct the fault.

What causes the fear of success? It could be caused by the depression that might come after a loss, or it could even result from the exhilaration accompanying a win. Both circumstances could create negative thoughts about winning.

Winning represents a major change in the status of a competitor; essentially he or she is now a WINNER instead of a NON-WINNER.

But what does that change in status really mean? It is this change in status that is at the root of the fear of success. Public expectations for winners are vastly different than they are for non-winners. And personal expectations by winners, of themselves, are different than they are for non-winners. Exploring these changes in status and expectations will give us some clues as to why the fear of success is as prevalent as it appears to be.

Public expectation of winners places a heavy burden on those who are successful. The public may expect you to win every tournament you enter, or at least to make a good showing. Every non-win could be interpreted as a loss or a failure to reach expectations. This added pressure of being expected to win may cause you to perform poorly. Thus, you may subconsciously fear success because of the added pressures and expectations that would be placed upon your shoulders.

Public expectations are far less for non-winners than for winners. Non-winners are NOT expected to win any event they enter. There is no public pressure to play up to any level of expectation. Some people prefer to remain within the "safety of the crowd". They may prefer to be close to the limelight, but not in it. There is a comfortable, secure feeling when you are NOT number one.

Responsibilities and expectations are heaped upon winners, even though they may not want them. These burdens can be threatening to someone who is not able to bring their self-image in line with their achievements.

Many successful people feel insecure because they do not think their success is a result of their own efforts. They are afraid their success has been caused by other reasons, thus they may not be able to repeat their successes. They are afraid that someone will "find them out", and they will be stripped of their success. David Niven, the highly successful actor, stated that he always feared that someone would "tap him on the shoulder and tell him that he had been found out".

The more successful you are, the more the public will expect success from you. This added pressure to perform at a high level often makes such performance more difficult to achieve. Thus, success sometimes makes further success more difficult. Even the person himself may put unnecessary pressure upon himself to perform at an unrealistically high level. A winner may feel that he or she must win each time to prove that the title of "winner" is merited. No such pressure or expectation exists for the non-winner.

Winning may create a situation for you that you do not desire. You may be required to make an acceptance speech, and the thought of having to do that may subconsciously prevent you from winning. Winning could cause you to have to make public appearances, and you could be deathly afraid of making public speeches. Losing eliminates these possible fears.

Winning can also make such a change in your status that you will get LESS (not more) publicity. Every sport has its highly qualified performer who, for some unexplained reason, cannot seem to win. The person performs very well on a regular basis, but just not well enough to win. Tom Kite was such a person in golf. Ernie Schlegel was such a person in bowling, always performing well enough to win large amounts of money but not well enough to take the title. Some writers suggested that Ernie subconsciously did not want to win since that would take away the one distinction he had, the highest money winner without a title. (He would then get less publicity.) Both Kite and Schlegel may have suffered from the fear of winning. Both are now winners, so the question is moot.

Ironically, once Schlegel won his first title, the second one took less than a month. It may have been that once he became a winner, the fear of success no longer had such a hold on him. Of course, he may not have suffered from the fear of success at all.

Charlie Tapp and Gil Sliker are two other competent performers who were non-winners for a long time. Tapp was the first to break through to the winners circle. Sliker became a winner within a month of Tapp's win. Was there some connection?

The fear of success is related to a fear of being noticed, a fear of being in the public eye. If you win you will be noticed and you will become somewhat of a public figure. The public will follow your performances. Many people do not like being on exhibit each time they compete. (Others love such a situation!) Those with the fear of being in the public eye often exhibit symptoms of the fear of success. Before these people can become truly successful, they have to overcome this fear of the public.

The fear of success also manifests itself in the form of a discrepancy between your accomplishments and your self-image. A person who thinks of himself as a winner, and wins, has a healthy self-image that is consistent with his achievements. But if he thinks of himself as a non-winner, and wins, a gap exists between his self-image and his accomplishments. This gap should be resolved. Hopefully, he can modify his self-image to agree with his achievements. In fact, imagining yourself as a winner is one of the best ways to bring about that success. (This subject is covered in Section 16, YOUR WONDERFUL IMAGINATION.)

Thus, the fear of success is strongly tied to the strength of your self-image. If your self-image is weak, then you may feel that you do not deserve any successes, and the fear of success could prevent you from winning. A strong self-image will allow you to achieve and accept success. Until you learn to feel that you deserve to win, it will be difficult to become a winner.

The fear of success suggests the concept of a PUBLIC FRAUD. Some people who do succeed are afraid that they have achieved success for reasons other than their capabilities and performances. They feel, subconsciously, that they have perpetuated some fraud on the public, and that this fraud is going TO BE EXPOSED.

If they do not achieve any further successes, maybe their imaginary fraud will never be exposed. (The David Niven example given above illustrates this concept.) Non-successful people have no such fears of exposure, since they have nothing to be exposed.

The fear of success may be more of a factor for the female athlete than for the male competitor. For a male, winning only serves to reinforce his masculinity, his male image. For a female, winning goes against her image as a woman; she may fear that she is losing her femininity.

A woman feels the need to retain all her feminine traits: non-aggressiveness, delicacy, submissiveness, gentleness, etc. If a woman competes and wins, she is often judged as less of a woman. This attitude on the part of competitors and spectators (men and women alike) is one that must be overcome if women are to gain equal status in the sports world. The concept that the man should win, that he has a right to win, and is embarrassed if he loses to a woman, is one that must be changed if women are to gain equality of treatment in the sports field.

However, the definition of the male image is closely tied to sports. One book, JOCK, equates the image of the male with that of sports: males must prove their masculinity in the competitive arena of sports. The characteristics required for success in a sport almost define a man. There is less possibility of a conflict, a subconscious fear of success, in the mind of a male athlete than in the mind of a female.

Thus, a woman who is successful in a sport is viewed as less feminine, as more masculine. The desire not to win, the fear of success, may be viewed as a subconscious desire to remain feminine. (How many women have played a game at less than their full potential in order to let their male competitor "save face"? Isn't this kind of behavior taught to females at the youngest of ages?)

The role for which a male is reared is consistent with what is considered necessary to excel in sports (aggressive and competitive). The role for which women are reared (submissive and cooperative) is inconsistent with these sports-related characteristics. So, the possibility for a mental conflict or dilemma exists far more strongly in the mind of the female than in the mind of the male. But, what if you are a female, and you wish to be or are successful? How can you increase your chances for success?

A technique called "displacement" is often used. The idea behind displacement is to convince yourself that you are NOT the one who is winning, someone else or some other group deserves the successes you are having. You are simply THE VEHICLE by which they are winning. Women can ascribe their good luck to the fact that they are doing what they can to advance the goals of women in general. If you are a member of a minority group, you can claim that your efforts are for that group. You can even give credit to the state you represent in competition.

The mental process of displacement allows you to free yourself from possible fears of success, because you are not the one who is winning, it is the group you represent.

Guilt is often a source of the fear of success. This guilt complex may take many forms. One is related to hero worship. Often a person will subconsciously not want to overshadow the feats of some person whom they have admired for a long time. For example, someone bowling Earl Anthony, who has admired Earl for a long time, may subconsciously not want to beat his hero. To do so would be disrespectful. (I bet Earl would like to face more bowlers with this problem.)

The solution to this hero-worship source of the fear of success is to psych yourself up to the point that you think you deserve a chance to establish new records, or to defeat those whose records you have admired. You need to de-venerate your heros, remove them from their pedestals. You need to develop a "scorn" for all records, and record holders. This will help you believe that you have every right to beat such records.

Still another source of guilt is often associated with one's parents. If your parents want you to follow one career, and you have decided to become a professional bowler, you may harbor a subconscious fear of succeeding in your profession instead of the one they preferred for you. The subconscious feeling is one of being disrespectful, disobedient to your parents. This feeling is more pronounced if they have indicated that you could not become a winner as a bowler. Winning proves them wrong, and adults are usually reluctant to prove their parents wrong. (Too bad children cannot have such an attitude.)

The solution to this source of the fear of success is to talk the situation out with the parents. Try to get them to understand your feelings. If they do, it may release you from the subconscious guilt feeling that you are going against them if you win.

Yet another source of the fear of success, associated with guilt feelings, is the person who equates winning with inflicting some injury or harm on the opponent, either physical or mental. (This could obviously be a big drawback for a professional boxer!) With bowling, you are more concerned with mental harm since it is not a physical contact sport. The person suffering this source of the fear of success thinks that he is embarrassing his opponents by beating them. This type of subconscious guilt feeling may restrict the normal competitive urges, and make it difficult to win.

There are many ways to overcome this source of guilt. One technique is to divert your feelings to the pins. Imagine that you are not bowling against your competitor; you are bowling against the pins: get aggressive towards them. This allows you to forget about the impact your win will have on your competitor. Since the pins are inanimate, are not human, it is easier to hold some form of aggression towards them. Few people feel sorry for the pins.

Another technique, but of questionable value, is to try to win by a small margin. The advisability of such a strategy is questionable at best, requiring the ability to ease up when it is necessary and score well when required.

Transferring your aggression to the pins helps you develop what has been termed the "killer instinct". Such a mental approach is healthy if your aggression is directed at the pins and not at your opponent. If you can keep your mind on your job of knocking pins down, and ignore thoughts of beating your competitor, you should not develop this particular mental fault associated with the fear of success.

Still another way to relieve yourself of the guilt associated with beating your opponent is to refuse to take credit for the win. You can credit luck. You can say you are doing it for your parents, for your team, for the fans, etc. You are saying to yourself (a self-deception) that it was not you who won. It was someone else. And, if it was someone else who won, then there is no reason for you to feel guilty. Such mental deception has been known to work, since it lets you DISASSOCIATE YOURSELF FROM the win. As with every form of self-deception, the criterion as to whether it should be used or not is simple: does it work for you?

Most bowlers, however, perform best when they look at the opponent as the enemy. They rile themselves to the point that it gets the adrenalin flowing freely. They use this viewpoint of their opponent, their enemy, to psych themselves up. They take the energy created by the imagined hostility and channel it into superior performance.

After the match is over, however, you should erase such thoughts from your mind and view the opponent as someone you respect for his or her talent, a worthy competitor, a compatriot in the sport. Think that you were both vying for the same prize, a win, and that only one could get the win. A healthy spirit of competition is most important in producing a winning attitude, and in overcoming the fear of success.

GUILTLESS WINNING should be your objective. When you begin to feel sorry for your opponent, during the competition, you may run the risk of the fear of success. To overcome this handicap, and it is a handicap, try to remove thoughts of your competitor from your mind. This is particularly important when you happen to be competing with someone whom you like, your roommate, your doubles partner, etc. You may have difficulty psyching yourself to the proper level for competition. Focusing your attention on the pins can help you reach the proper competitive level

Sometimes wanting to win too badly is mistaken for the fear of success. When you want to win too badly, you may concentrate too hard on winning, instead of trying to concentrate on what is necessary to win. Section 5, LET IT HAPPEN NATURALLY, stressed the idea that you should not think about winning, that you should think only about executing each shot as well as you can.

Trying to win too badly makes the win more difficult to achieve, and you may be judged as having the mental fault of the fear of success.

The way to minimize the impact of the fear of success is to recognize exactly what it is. You need information about yourself and your motivations, which can only come about by examination and self study. If the pattern of success and failure which has been programmed into your life has created a tendency toward this fear of success, then you have to come to grips with the situation. This is not any different than facing any other mental problem preventing you from achieving an optimum mental game. Recognize the problem and develop a plan of attack to minimize its effect or eliminate the problem.

TO DENY THE EXISTENCE OF THE FEAR OF SUCCESS MAKES IT NO LESS REAL. If you have the problem, denying its existence will not make it disappear. Take a very close and objective look at your mental game. If you are harboring even the slightest doubts about being successful, you could be keeping yourself from reaching your full potential.

Some people succeed even though they have the fear of success deeply embedded in their subconscious mind. With others, the fear prevents them from ever reaching their full potential. Those who do succeed, will do so because their need to succeed, their desire to win, is far stronger than their fear of success. The stronger your desire to win, the more capable you are of overcoming the fear of success.

The fear of success is an involved topic. If you are interested in exploring the subject in greater detail, you should read the book entitled THE FEAR OF SUCCESS, listed in the Bibliography.

Winners have a positive self-image.

--- WINNERS HAVE A POSITIVE SELF-IMAGE. THEY EXPECT TO WIN. ---

"The individual's own personality is the major obstacle to the attainment of competence", states Stuart H. Walker in his book, WINNING (The Psychology of Winning). This statement summarizes the theme of this entire book. Whether a person ever becomes a winner will depend upon his ability to conquer the mental game within himself. Winners have a winning attitude and a winning personality. They expect to win.

However, if you were to ask a number of winners what it was that allowed them to win, you would find a wide range of answers. Certainly, the physical competence of the particular sport would be necessary, but the mental game would be cited as the factor which allows them to take full advantage of their physical game. Many competent athletes do not reach their full potential because of their mental game.

This entire book has focused on the mental game. Therefore, in this concluding chapter I will assume that you have the physical or technical competence to perform at a high level, and limit this discussion to additional parts of the mental game.

Many aspects of the mental game have been discussed in considerable depth in various sections of this book. That material will not be repeated here, although it is obvious that I feel that these are necessary parts of every winner's mental game.

For example, a winner is in control of his or her emotions during competition, is able to relax and concentrate at all times, enjoys competition, knows the value of good physical health, has a healthy attitude towards luck, has developed subconscious competence, trusts the subconscious to deliver the ball, can psych himself up, down, or in as required, can avoid being psyched-out, develops his natural talents, recognizes and tries to correct any attitude or knowledge faults, has a good imagination, and has no fear of success, etc.

In this final section, I will elaborate on five mental traits or characteristics which I feel are the most important traits for any competitor to have if he or she is to develop a winner's personality. These five are interrelated, but I have separated them for ease in presentation. The five are: (1) a positive self-image, (2) determination and desire to win, (3) self-confidence, (4) a setting of realistic goals, and (5) a willingness to learn.

WINNERS HAVE A POSITIVE SELF-IMAGE: Winners think of themselves as winners. Winners have a self-image that allows them to win, it does not stop them from achieving their full potential. They have no mental or psychological blocks which would interfere with their performance. It may be that a positive self-image is the most important mental trait of consistent winners. So many other characteristics are only possible if you have a strong and positive image of yourself. If you do not have such an image, it is very difficult if not impossible to develop the other characteristics. THE MIND SETS THE LIMITS WITHIN WHICH THE BODY CAN ACHIEVE.

Imagination is the key to developing a positive self-image. As mentioned in Section 16, YOUR WONDERFUL IMAGINATION, it is possible to produce changes in your attitude and personality by sheer force of your imagination. A statement heard many times in the PBA school I attended summed it up very nicely: "Our thoughts develop our personalities". Since you have the option to think either positive or negative thoughts about yourself, why not choose positive thoughts?

Unless you are able to develop a positive image about yourself, it is not possible to use the many techniques for developing a positive attitude. YOUR SELF-IMAGE MUST BE CONSISTENT WITH YOUR THOUGHTS; it WILL BE CONSISTENT with your thoughts. If your image of yourself is predominately negative, then this negative image will prevent you from incorporating positive thoughts into your attitudes and personality. First, develop the positive self-image; then you have removed most of the obstacles from your path to success.

If you want to read the best book on creating a positive self-image, read Maxwell Maltz's book, THE MAGIC POWER OF SELF-IMAGE PSYCHOLOGY. His other book, PSYCHO-CYBERNETICS also gives specific guidelines for developing your successful self-image.

WINNERS HAVE THE DESIRE AND DETERMINATION TO WIN: When noted bowling writer Chuck Pezzano asked Earl Anthony what made him a consistent winner, Earl answered: "I guess I just want to win more than the other guy." Of course Earl's physical ability to roll the ball the same way (like a robot), has a lot to do with his success. Still, it is doubtful if he could have achieved the greatest winning record in bowling if he did not have a strong desire to win.

Simple desire is certainly not enough to produce a consistent winner. That desire must be converted into a persistence that makes one never give up, never give the competitor an edge, never give anything less than your best in every competition. Desire must be converted into a strong commitment to becoming a winner, doing all that is necessary to transfer desire into a tough, competitive mental attitude.

Strong desire can be called determination. Determination describes a person who has an extremely high endurance level; one who enjoys long practice sessions as long as skill development is being achieved; one who keeps himself in top physical and mental form in preparation for competition; a person who does not give up, who will give every available ounce of effort towards winning. Tell a determined person he cannot do something, and that person will redouble his efforts instead of conceding defeat.

When determined individuals are faced with adversity, with roadblocks, a setback or disaster, you can expect from them an effort that is more than they would normally exert. In other words, they become more determined when obstacles are in their way. They do not shy away from problems; they attack them. Despite a normally high effort level, an even greater effort is exerted when it is needed. Those less determined would give in to the obstacles.

Determination takes confidence in your abilities, but also PRODUCES confidence. You are more likely to succeed with the proper amount of determination, and each success creates a more confident feeling that you can be successful again.

Desire and determination are strong mental characteristics. These two factors, combined with a positive self-image, may be the most important traits for producing a winning mental game. So many other aspects of the game depend upon these traits.

WINNERS ARE SELF-CONFIDENT: Having self-confidence means believing in yourself and in your capabilities. It is a personal feeling that you are capable of performing at a high skill level. Self-confidence is, as are all these mental characteristics, inter-related with other aspects of the attitude and personality of a winner.

A positive self-image is based upon confidence, and also produces confidence. Desire and determination lead to success, which also produces self-confidence. Thus, these first three mental traits are closely related, and it is easy to become confused as to which one precedes the other. But, fortunately the answer to that question is not necessary to the development of a sound mental game.

Self-confidence must not lead to cockiness, which is an inflated sense of one's abilities. Self-confidence must be realistic, based upon an objective and realistic assessment of your capabilities.

A confident attitude is also a good strategy to use in competition. When faced with a confident competitor, some bowlers give up, are too quick to concede defeat.

Confidence in yourself gives you the assurance that you will be able to rise to any occasion, to handle any competitive situation. When a situation arises that might produce anxiety, your confidence in your abilities will let you handle that situation with the least amount of anxiety..

Self-confidence is the best defense against an attack of nerves. The likelihood of a "choke" in a clutch situation is reduced in proportion to the amount of confidence you have. The more confidence you have, the less likely you are to choke under pressure. The less confidence you have, the more likely you are to execute a bad shot under pressure.

Self-confidence can lead to courageous performances. Someone who is confident in his or her abilities will take chances when necessary. For example, eventual tournament winner Mal Acosta changed from the extreme outside line to the extreme inside line in the final frames of a championship match. This courageous move paid off. A less courageous person might not have made the dramatic move, and would probably not have won. Mal had the confidence in his abilities.

Professional golfer Jerry Pate can trace his entire career success to one courageous 5-iron shot to the final green which gave him the title to the U.S. Open. It was an all-or-nothing shot with a huge lake hazard, that a less confident or less courageous competitor might not have been able to execute.

James Archer, a frequent speaker at the PBA School, listed FIVE WAYS TO BUILD YOUR SELF-CONFIDENCE: (1) Like yourself (develop a positive self-image; (2) Keep growing (keep improving both your mental and physical game); (3) Become your best (be progressively dissatisfied, don't stop improving); (4) Act confident (maintain an air of confidence that is realistic, and in line with your personal capabilities); and (5) Be willing to change (be constantly aware of areas for personal improvement).

Fear is the enemy of confidence. Robinson, in his book, MIND IN THE MAKING, states that "fear is the result of ignorance and uncertainty. Confidence comes from experience and knowledge." To conquer fear, to develop confidence, follow Ralph Waldo Emerson's advice: " Do the thing you fear and the death of fear is certain".

WINNERS SET REALISTIC GOALS: Winners set goals or targets for themselves. These goals might be related to: physical skills, methods of practice, personal mental growth, competitive achievements, etc.

Setting goals for yourself is a useful means of preparing for success and winning. These goals should be realistic and reachable, but sufficiently high to stretch your mind and body. Goals should represent standards of performance against which you can judge your current level of performance. Goal-oriented behavior is an important part of a winner's mental game.

Goal-setting is a continuous process. As your skill level rises, you must adjust your goals upwards to new levels. Higher goals call for higher skill levels. Keep elevating your goals to levels which represent a sufficient challenge for your skills, yet realistic enough that they can eventually be achieved.

THE ACT OF GOAL-SETTING GENERATES THE ENERGY TO REACH THE GOAL. If you feel very tired, but suddenly have something that you really want to do, your wanting to do it badly enough will overcome the tiredness. You somehow get the energy to put the idea into effect. The goal has generated the energy to reach it.

A person who is not committed enough to the development of his or her talents to express those commitments in the form of specific goals, is probably not willing to spend the time preparing a mental game that will lead to maximum performance. A firm commitment to excellence is needed if one is to achieve that level of competence.

Goal-setting aids in that developmental process.

WINNERS ARE WILLING TO LEARN: Although it is easy to learn how to roll a ball down the lane, it is impossible to master the game. Neither the physical nor the mental game is ever developed to the point that no further development is possible. Personal learning and growth are ongoing processes; there is no end.

A winning mental attitude recognizes this endless educational process and looks for opportunities to learn. This does not mean that a winner is dissatisfied with his present level of knowledge, but it does mean that he is willing to admit that there is still more for him to learn. Many people stop their growth and progress by the mistaken assumption that they have learned all they need to learn. Few people will admit that they have mastered the mental game, but a large number actually feel that they have mastered the physical game.

A healthier mental attitude is one of progressive dissatisfaction with the current state of knowledge. That is, a winner is content with the current level of knowledge, but wants to progress to an even higher level. There is always room for improvement, but there needs to be a sense of satisfaction with what has already been learned and achieved.

Competitors who are PROGRESSIVELY dissatisfied are not really dissatisfied with the current level of competence and success they have achieved; but they are dissatisfied enough to want to achieve still higher levels. They set higher goals for themselves, to keep them in this achievement-oriented frame of mind.

Complacency is avoided by progressive dissatisfaction. If you are too satisfied with your current skill level, then you will not likely improve much beyond it. On the other hand, you do not want to become too dissatisfied with your progress to date. This might cause you to become discouraged and give up on reaching new heights.

Accepting responsibility for your actions is the first, but very important, step towards continuous learning. Bowling has, unfortunately, an alibi-oriented language. There are too many excuses or alibis for poor performance: I had the wrong equipment; It wasn't my condition; I was tapped; I never get any luck; I missed my spot; I chopped: The pins are too heavy, too light; I never score well in this house; etc. Unless you are able to accept complete responsibility for what happens, to recognize when you have bowled badly and when you have bowled well, there is very little chance for you to improve your game.

You must admit and recognize your shortcomings if you ever hope to reach your full potential. Look at them as excellent possibilities for growth, not personal defects or failings. Those who cannot recognize their shortcomings, or who fail to accept responsibility for them, have no chance to correct them.

In conclusion, these five mental characteristics or traits are extremely important aspects of any successful mental game: a positive self-image; determination and desire to win; self-confidence; setting realistic goals; and willingness to learn. Combining these five traits with the many others mentioned throughout the book, should give you an outline for a mental game that will meet all your requirements.

Mental traits are intangible and hard to measure. Nevertheless, they represent standards or goals against which you can compare your current mental game. If you want a mental game that will allow you to fully utilize your physical game, you will have to pay special attention to these well-established traits of winners.

Your personality, your self-image, your attitudes and temperament, define the limits of your mental growth. THERE ARE NO PRACTICAL LIMITS TO YOUR MENTAL GROWTH; ONLY THOSE THAT YOU PLACE ON YOURSELF. As you expand your mental game, you expand the limits of your performance.

Development of your personality, your mental game, is completely within your control. Winners recognize this, and take full responsibility for their performance. Your ultimate level of success is in your hands. And, if you are going to put your fate in someone's hands, why not make them your own?

Allen, George and Ritger, Dick: THE ENCYCLOPEDIA OF BOWLING INSTRUCTION, Tempe Publishers, Inc., Box 28262, Tempe, AZ., 85282. 1982

Benson, Herbert,M.D.: THE RELAXATION RESPONSE, William Morrow & Co., New York, 1975

Carr, A.H.Z.: HOW TO ATTRACT GOOD LUCK, Wilshire Book Co., No. Hollywood, CA, 1978

Clark, Nancy,MS.,R.D.: THE ATHLETE'S KITCHEN, Bantam Book, New York, NY, 1983

Curtis, Donald: YOUR THOUGHTS CAN CHANGE YOUR LIFE, Wilshire Book Co., No. Hollywood, CA, 1973

Downs, Hugh: POTENTIAL: The Way to Emotional Maturity, Doubleday & Co., Inc., Garden City, NY, 1973

Gallwey, W. Timothy: THE INNER GAME OF GOLF, Random House, Inc., New York, NY, 1979

Gallwey, W. Timothy: THE INNER GAME OF TENNIS, Random House, Inc., New York, NY, 1974

Glasser, William: POSITIVE ADDICTION, Harper & Row Publishers, New York, NY, 1976

Heise, Jack: BOWL BETTER USING SELF-HYPNOSIS, Wilshire Book Co., No. Hollywood, CA, 1979

Jerome, John: THE SWEET SPOT IN TIME, Avon Books, Hearst Corporation, New York, NY, 1982

Karlins, Marvin and Andrews, Lewis M.: BIOFEEDBACK, Warner Communications Co., New York, NY, 1975

Kauss, David R.: PEAK PERFORMANCE, Prentice-Hall, Inc., Englewood Cliffs, NJ, 1980

Lager, Lance and Kraft, Amy L.: MENTAL JUDO, Crown Publishers Inc., New York, NY, 1981

Maltz, Maxwell: THE MAGIC POWER OF SELF-IMAGE PSYCHOLOGY, Pocket Books, Simon & Schuster, New York, NY, 1970

Maltz, Maxwell: PSYCHO-CYBERNETICS, Simon & Schuster, Inc., New York, NY, 1960

Marcus, Jay B.: TM AND BUSINESS, McGraw-Hill Book Co., New York, NY, 1977

Peale, Norman Vincent: THE POWER OF POSITIVE THINKING, Prentice-Hall, Inc., New York, 1952.

Petrie, Sidney and Stone, Robert B.: HYPNO-CYBERNETICS, New American Library, Inc., New York, NY, 1976

Sabo, Donald F. and Runfola, Ross: JOCK: SPORTS AND MALE IDENTITY, Prentice-Hall, Inc., Englewood Cliffs, NJ, 1980

Scott, Michael D. and Pelliccioni,Jr., Louis: DON'T CHOKE: HOW ATHLETES CAN BECOME WINNERS, Prentice-Hall, Inc., Englewood Cliffs, NJ, 1982

Tec, Leon: THE FEAR OF SUCCESS, Harper & Row Publishers, New York, NY, 1978

Tutko, Thomas and Tosh, Umberto: SPORTS PSYCHING: Playing Your Best Game All of the Time, J.P. Tarcher, Inc., Los Angeles, CA, 1976

Walker, Stuart H.: WINNING: THE PSYCHOLOGY OF COMPETITION, W.W. Norton & Co., New York, NY, 1980

Werthman, Michael: SELF-PSYCHING, J.P. Tarcher, Inc., Los Angeles, CA, 1978